9·99

RELEASE

SMALL BUSINESS

WRITING A PRESS RELEASE

How to get the right kind of publicity and news coverage

Peter Bartram

3rd edition

How To Books

Cartoons by Mike Flanagan

British Library cataloguing-in-publication data

A catalogue record for this book is available from the British Library.

Published by How To Books Ltd,
3 Newtec Place, Magdalen Road,
Oxford OX4 1RE, United Kingdom
Tel: (01865) 793806. Fax: (01865) 248780
email: info@howtobooks.co.uk
www.howtobooks.co.uk

First published 1993
Second edition 1995
Third edition 1999

Note: The material contained in this book is set out in good faith for
general guidance and no liability can be accepted for loss or expense
incurred as a result of relying in particular circumstances on statements
made in the book. The law and regulations are complex and liable to
change, and readers should check the current position with the relevant
authorities before making personal arrangements.

Cover design Shireen Nathoo Design
Cover image PhotoDisc

Produced for How To Books by Deer Park Productions.
Typeset by Concept Communications Ltd, Crayford, Kent.
Printed and bound by The Cromwell Press, Trowbridge, Wiltshire.

Preface

to the Third Edition

This is the third edition of a book – previously published as *How to Write a Press Release* – which has already helped thousands of press officers to get their press releases into print. It has been completely updated and some new material has been added.

Getting the right kind of publicity and news coverage can be vital for all kinds of organisations, both in the private and, increasingly, throughout the public sector. Every day, newspapers and magazines are deluged with thousands of press releases, the vast majority of which end up in the bin. Why do so few make it into print? What really makes an editor sit up and take notice? Which are the key factors that spell oblivion for so much material, while some organisations seem almost certain to guarantee valuable press coverage for themselves?

The aim of this book is to take you step-by-step through every stage of the process of writing a press release, from conceiving your story idea, researching the information and writing the release, to distributing it by the most effective means. Adopting a more professional approach will benefit many organisations which may currently be losing out despite having an important and interesting story to tell.

Peter Bartram

List of Illustrations

Contents

1
Hitting the Headlines

'When a dog bites a man that is not news, but when a man bites a dog, that is news.' — John B. Bogart (1845-1920), US journalist.

THE POWER OF MEDIA COVERAGE

Does the media have power? And, if it does, exactly what form does that power take? To answer these questions, let us first consider some rather important statistics:

- More than 85 per cent of the population of the UK watches **television** every day.

- More than 40 per cent of the population reads at least one daily **newspaper**.

- More than 70 per cent of the population listens to the **radio** for at least one hour every day.

- There are more than 11,000 regular **newspapers and magazines** in the UK with a combined circulation of more than 100 million.

The answers lie in those statistics. Yes: the media does have power through its pervasive character. It reaches everywhere. But it is the power to influence and persuade, rather than the power to direct.

Because we can have first-hand knowledge of only a comparatively few people, places, companies, institutions and so on, most of our knowledge of the world comes through the media. But the media does not only provide us with information in a dispassionate and objective way. It shapes our perception of people and institutions through the way it presents the information. It does this in three main ways:

●   Through the subjects it puts in and the subjects it chooses to leave
    out.

●   By the general tone of the way it presents subjects.

●   By the comments and arguments it makes about the subjects it deals
    with.

No wonder, then, that organisations of all kinds and all sizes seek to
shape what is written or broadcast about them in the media. And in doing
that they use many techniques, generally grouped under the term **public
relations**. In this book, we are not concerned with the full and varied
repertoire of public relations techniques. Instead, we focus on just one:
the press release.

USES AND ABUSES OF THE PRESS RELEASE

The press release (or **news release** as some prefer to call it) is probably
the single most widely used technique for providing information to the
media. It has many advantages:

●   It is cheap.
●   It does not take much time to produce.
●   It is (seemingly) simple.

And yet the press release is one of the most abused of all techniques
used by organisations to reach the media. Every day, sackfuls of press
releases cascade on to journalists' desks. A national newspaper could
well receive 1,000, a popular trade or technical magazine anything from
100 to 200. Even a freelance journalist could receive as many as 20 or
30 a day.

Most are never used. They end up on the spike – that fearsome imple-
ment upon which journalists impale unwanted copy – or in the bin. Even
worse, most never stood a chance of being used. They should never have
been sent, and probably not written. The trees used in the manufacture
of the paper and the envelopes gave up their lives in vain.

Yet, properly used, the press release can be a highly effective way of
getting your message across to the media. And although journalists generally decry the torrent of releases that land on their desks, they still scan
through them looking for rare newsworthy nuggets among the all-too-
plentiful dross. This book is all about providing press releases:

- that get used;

- that provide useful and effective information about your organisation;

- that help to shape journalists' perceptions and feelings for your organisation and thus, through them, the perceptions and feelings of the wider public.

Producing a press release that achieves these objectives requires certain specific skills and a certain amount of common sense.

The skills can certainly be learned, although the common sense might be a little harder to acquire. But by the end of the book, the attentive reader should be equipped with both and ready to send out releases that really will hit the headlines.

Problem
Some of our managers say we need the skills of a public relations consultancy to put out press releases. As we can't afford a consultancy's fancy fees, we've written off press relations.

Remedy
Write it back in. You don't need to pay the high fees often demanded by PR consultants in order to send out effective press releases. (Indeed, many of the press releases put out by PR consultants fall far short of what is needed.) Read on and find out how you become an effective press officer yourself.

WHAT MAKES A PRESS RELEASE WORK?

A truly successful press release generally contains the right story in the right place at the right time. That may sound as though there is a strong element of luck in the process of your release finding its way into the media. Yes, there is some luck in it. For example, you could have sent a strong story that might have made a couple of columns on a slow news day. Except that your story arrived the day the Bill Clinton–Monica Lewinsky story broke, and the paper has cleared 10 pages for coverage, leaving room for only the most essential other items.

However, there is an adage that lucky people make their own luck. And this is as true of winning media coverage from press releases as any other business activity. (We shall look at how to find stories that score with the media in Chapter 4.)

Basic requirements

In the meantime, let us look at some of the basics without which your press release is likely to slide straight into the bin. In order to give your release even a chance of success you need to make sure it is:

- *Relevant*
  Sounds obvious, but most releases are fired out in blanket mailings which annoy journalists, achieve nothing for the sender and only provide extra revenue for the Royal Mail.

- *Focused*
  Less obvious, but equally important. In many cases the topic of a release will arouse a journalist's interest which will be dashed because he can't find the information in the release that he needs to write a story for his publication. In other words, the topic is right, but the treatment is wrong. We will be coming back to this point in Chapter 3.

- *Timely*
  Today's newspaper is tomorrow's fish and chip wrapping. Too often organisations sit on 'stories' that would have made it in print weeks ago, but are now just too old and tired to warrant the description 'news'.

- *Readable*
  Even the hottest story will flop if it is poorly written, hidden in a mass of verbiage or tied up in jargon. The main facts of the story need to be clearly and logically presented. (We will come back to this in detail in Chapters 5 and 6.)

- *Presentable*
  The press release needs to look as though it contains some interesting information. That means it has to be set out like a news story and clearly printed in readable type. A simple point, but it is surprising how many releases fail this test. (We shall look at this issue thoroughly in Chapter 6.)

Above all, the press release needs one final quality. The most important quality of all. It needs to be *news*. But this raises an even more important question. Just what *is* news?

Action point

If you have already issued some press releases, take another look at them. How do they stand up against the relevant, focused, timely, readable, presentable criteria? Take one of your previous releases and rate it against each of the five criteria on a scale of one to five, where five equals 'precisely what's needed' and one equals 'way off beam'. Then turn to the end of the chapter to see how your release scored.

WHAT IS NEWS?

Lord Northcliffe, the founder of the *Daily Mail*, said: 'News is what somebody somewhere wants to suppress; all the rest is advertising.' That could certainly be taken as a credo for an investigative journalist, but it is not a suitable definition for all media. Nor is it suitable for a press release writer.

Harold Evans, former campaigning editor of the *Sunday Times*, came a little closer in his book *The Practice of Journalism* (Heinemann, 1963): 'News is people. It is people talking and people doing. Committees and Cabinets and courts are people; so are fires, accidents and planning decisions. They are only news because they involve and affect people.' And, backing up that theme, Arthur Christensen, probably the greatest ever editor of the *Daily Express*, instructed his reporters: 'Always, always, always, tell the story through people.'

A common theme of all these quotations is **people**. So news must be about people, connected to people or affect people in some way. In fact, too often, press release writers fail to stress the people aspect of their story. Yet if you dig deeply enough there is always a 'people angle' and almost every press release is strengthened by finding it.

USING COMMON NEWS THEMES

If you look at the stories in the media, you will find a number of common themes. You should consider these themes when writing your press releases.

Using important events

Big stories are important. They are something that people have to know about. The outbreak of a war, the result of an election, the sinking of a ship are all important events that people will want to know about. In many cases, they are events that will directly affect people's lives.

In the business world, there are also important events. The Bank of

England raising or lowering interest rates, BT putting down telephone charges, the IBA handing out independent TV franchises are all events that affect millions of people's lives.

Does this mean that news has to be nationally 'important'? Not necessarily. The 'news' that your organisation can provide may not be important to the whole country, but it could be significant to groups of people. If you open a new factory or shop, that will be big news in the town where it happens. If you replace one product line with another, that will be significant news to those who use the product.

The lesson: when what your organisation does has an impact on the lives of a significant number of people you could be making news.

Action point
What 'important' news events happened in your organisation in the last year? Make a list. Did you use press releases to explain them to the media?

Using controversy
People love a good argument – especially when they can watch other people at it. So controversy often makes news. Politicians know this only too well. They use controversy as a tool to get themselves into the media. Your organisation could use controversy as a news-making tool. The checklist below suggests some ways.

Checklist: how you can use controversy to make news
● Attack a government decision.
● Call for higher safety standards.
● Demand a change of economic policy.
● Campaign for better customer service.
● Ask the council to help local business.
● Draw attention to unfair trade practices.
● Demand a better deal for small businesses.
● Make a prediction about the future.
● Suggest a new policy.

Using conflict
Just as controversy gets journalists writing, so does conflict. Even though conflict rather than amity seems to be the natural state of human condition, the media is fascinated by conflict. Sometimes, conflict springs from controversy, on other occasions from different causes. When you do the kind of things in the checklist below you could make news.

Checklist: events that create conflict and make news
- Fight for an elected office.
- Tussle for boardroom control.
- Contest a take-over battle.
- Fight for supremacy among competing technologies.
- Battle for greater market share.
- Cut prices.
- Open a rival branch.

Using novelty value

Anything unusual makes news. Ask yourself, 'what has our organisation got that nobody else has? What have we done that nobody has done before?' Like most other kinds of news an item that might make an editor go 'ho-hum' on one paper might tickle the fancy on another. The message: actively look for things that are new or unusual in your organisation.

Checklist: how you can use novelty to make news
- Announce the first.
- Reveal the oldest, the youngest.
- Show an unusual use for your product or service.
- Describe a coincidence.
- Highlight a chance event.
- Find a surprising fact or statistic.
- Say goodbye to the last.

Using empathy

Empathy — relating to the reader, understanding and sharing his problems — creates news. People are always keen to read articles that relate to their own lives. Editors are well aware of this. That is one reason why newspapers and consumer magazines have so many 'lifestyle' type articles about subjects like homes, food, clothes and so on.

In the trade or technical press, 'empathy' articles will normally relate to readers' working lives. Readers are interested in articles which provide useful information for their company or that will help them in their own careers.

Checklist: how to use empathy to make news
- Show how your product can help.
- Provide case studies on your service in action.
- List tips to handle a common problem.
- Describe the experience of your staff.
- Conduct a survey on the issues that concern people.

Suggested action

Consider how each of these news drivers — importance, controversy, conflict, novelty and empathy — could be used by your organisation.

1.   Which of the examples in the checklists could you use?
2.   Make some notes on how they could be adapted for your own use.
3.   Are there any examples not listed that you could use?

WHY NEWS DIFFERS FROM ONE PUBLICATION TO ANOTHER

Newspapers and magazines exist for two reasons — to serve their readers and make a profit for their owners. They achieve the second by fulfilling the first. So every editor worth his salt — whether of a national newspaper or a small trade and technical publication — will know a lot about his readers. Specifically, he will know:

● What kind of people they are (for example, the age profile, proportion of men to women, how many are professional, clerical, manual workers, and so on).

● Where they live (for example, are they spread across the country or do they live in one geographical area?)

● Why they read this publication (for example, is it for information, entertainment, work or pleasure, education or reference?)

   Drawing on that and other information will help the editor shape the kind of material he includes in his publication. And it is the main reason why what is 'news' differs so much from one newspaper or magazine to another.

Example 1

Let us illustrate this with two examples. First here are the main news stories that appeared on the business pages of some daily papers on one day:

● *Financial Times*: UK banks face £490m suit
● *Times*: More lenders back call for housing boost
● *Independent*: NatWest profits double despite loss on branches
● *Daily Mail*: Bad debts dog NatWest

- *Daily Mirror*: Don't be a tail of woe (story about dog insurance)
- *Daily Express*: Cold wind of recession blows north
- *The Sun*: Henlys workers backing Cowies

As you can see, there is a wide difference between them, reflecting the different readerships they serve.

Example 2

Another example reinforces the point. You might think that a woman's magazine is a woman's magazine is a woman's magazine. Not a bit of it. Today, the woman's magazine market is highly 'segmented'. This means that each is targeted at a specific portion of the female population. Here is this author's subjective analysis:

- *Woman's Realm*: for the middle-aged woman
- *Chat*: the secretary's coffee break companion
- *Elle*: for the sophisticated woman with cash in her purse
- *Options*: for the thirtysomethings
- *19*: for the teens and early twenties
- *Cosmopolitan*: for the sex-obsessed twenties
- *She*: for the educated career woman

The lesson from these two analyses is not to take a publication at face value. You need to look in more detail at the readers it serves and the way it serves them. All this means that as a press release writer you will need to understand some basic facts about the kind of news and information the different publications you are targeting will want. We deal with this in more detail in Chapter 3.

EDITORS' CRITERIA FOR 'NEWS'

Whether your story stands a chance of making it into the paper depends on a number of factors. The starting point is whether the editor (or news editor) considers it will be of interest to his readers. In making that judgement, he will use his knowledge about the profile of his readers, drawing on his criteria mentioned above.

Hard and soft news

However, in many publications — certainly national newspapers and the leading business or trade and technical publications — the fact that a story might interest a largish number of the readers is not enough to ensure it makes it into print. Of course, there are some stories — the fall of a government, a major disaster, a budget speech — that all papers will carry (although not in the same way). They are 'hard' news, important events or happenings that people cannot afford to ignore. These are what journalists call 'must' stories.

But there are plenty of stories that fall into the 'soft' news category. Soft news can best be described as something that is interesting but not world-stopping. In other words, if you didn't know about it, you wouldn't be out of touch. Daily newspapers carry an increasing number of soft news stories, because many of the hard news stories, which they must carry as 'journals of record', have already been broadcast on radio and TV. The choice of soft news and feature articles helps to give a paper its individual character. And it is in this area that you can often score as a creative press release writer. For more, see Chapter 4.

At the end of the day, editors want their own paper or magazine to be read. And, quite simply, the way to do that is to have material in it worth reading. Most editors interpret that to mean a fair number of stories that have not appeared elsewhere. Exclusives, if you like.

Much of a journalist's time is spent finding stories that are of interest to the readers and have not appeared in other papers. If you have a story that meets those criteria and can write it in a readable press release, you could be in business. But who do you give the story to?

HOW NEWSPAPERS COLLECT THE NEWS

Whether your press release leaps into print will partly depend on whether you have a strong story targeted at the right publication. But it could also partly hinge on where you feed it into the news gathering system. You need to find out where the news gathering 'pressure points' in your target publications are. The pressure points are those places in the publication's news gathering chain where you can feed in a press release. In searching out the pressure points, we need to look briefly at how news is gathered.

National newspapers
National newspapers have sophisticated news gathering machines. The main elements in them are:

●   **The news desk:** this is the main clearing desk for news which comes from many different sources. The news desk will be headed by:

- **The News editor**, in charge of the paper's home news gathering activities. He will be assisted by:

- **A copy taster**, who looks at each item from whatever source it arrives and decides whether it merits further attention by the news editor. A substantial proportion of stories are 'spiked' — newspaperese for discarded — by the copy taster.

It is worth noting that on most national newspapers there will be:

A foreign news editor
A business news editor
A sports news editor
A women's news editor

This pattern is repeated, normally without the foreign editor, and sometimes without the business editor, on regional daily and evening newspapers. News will arrive on the news desk from a variety of sources. These include:

Specialist correspondents
National newspapers have specialist reporters covering a large number of areas including business, fashion, motoring, gardening, wine, crime, politics, economic affairs, chess, medicine and a bewildering range of other specialist topics. The precise range of specialist reporters on any paper will depend on the shape of its coverage — in turn, driven by the readers it serves.

General assignment reporters
Newsroom-based story sleuths who will follow up a range of stories that can't be allocated to the specialist correspondents.

Stringers
Reporters 'strung out' in the main towns around the country whose job is to keep an eye open for stories in their area which could make the national press. They sometimes work for several papers and are often employed by specialist regional news agencies.

Wire services
These include the main syndicated news gathering organisations such as the **Press Association** (for home news) and **Reuters** (for foreign news), themselves largely owned by the national newspapers.

Press releases
These crash on to the news desk every day by the barrow-load. Most end on the spike.

Tip-offs
Phoned in by PR people or members of the public, often hoping for (and just occasionally receiving) some reward.

Finding the pressure points
As you will realise there are several points in this news gathering structure where you can feed in your press release. And part of the skill lies in knowing where.

One of the biggest mistakes made by the novice press release writer is to assume that all press releases should be sent to the editor. This is certainly not the case on national and regional newspapers, where the editor won't even see them. It is not even the case on a number of leading trade and technical publications, where news is collected and processed by journalists who specialise in different topics. The more precisely you target your release in this news gathering hierarchy, the more chance it stands of reaching a journalist who might be interested in the story.

Broadcasting
Finally, TV and radio. The news gathering machine of a major service such as Independent Television News is similar to that of a national newspaper. But there are many regional TV stations which have considerably smaller news gathering organisations. At local radio stations, the news service is often run by a handful of people who each have to cover a wide range of topics.

Tips for effective targeting
Here are a few tips to help you target the news gathering pressure points:

● On a small publication with a handful of editorial staff, send to the editor.

● On a larger publication send to the editor or news editor.

● If the publication has a specialist correspondent who regularly handles stories about your industry, send releases to him, unless he asks you to send them to the editor.

● On regional or local newspapers send the story to the local reporter covering your area.

● On a national newspaper, send to the news desk or a specialist correspondent, if appropriate.

● In some cases, you might make national coverage by feeding your story to the local 'stringer'.

Problem and remedy

Problem: I've sent press releases to specialist correspondents and they ask me to send them to the editor.

Remedy: They will, if the releases seem to be of little news value. If you can gain a reputation of being a source of really good stories, you will find their attitude changes. All journalists like to find regular sources of good stories. Make sure you send the best stories to the specialists.

HOW NEWS IS PROCESSED

Most editors are autocrats, but appreciate the importance of a highly motivated and talented team around them. On a national newspaper the core of this team comes together twice a day at the morning and evening conferences.

These conferences, attended by the senior editorial executives from different departments of the paper, are something of a legend in newspaper circles. They are said to be the battlefield where the soul of the paper is fought over. More prosaically, they are the forum in which the executives review possible stories and decide what gets into the paper. The executives also debate the relative importance to be given to different stories.

At the morning conference, the team will look at up-coming news events that day — what's happening in Parliament, who's up in court, where will the Royals be, etc. These are what are known in the paper as the 'diary' stories, events which every journalist knows are going to happen. The various department heads — news, foreign, sport and so on — will also reveal a little of the off-diary stories they hope to net during the day. These are the stories which they hope will be exclusives for their own paper and which have been dug out by their own reporters.

At the evening conference, the team will look at what stories will be available, how they shape up in relative news value, and the prominence that ought to be given to the main ones.

Do stories discussed at these conferences ever start life as a press release? Not often, but it does happen and as a shrewd release strategist, if you get your story onto the agenda at one of the conferences you are generally talking big coverage — but then you will need the story to match it.

If your story does not make the conference — and 999 times out of 1,000 it will not — it will pass through a number of stages before reaching the paper. The process described here operates on national and regional newspapers. The process on magazines is similar but you may find the same people doing several jobs.

Four steps into print

Press release writers sometimes complain that what they write is completely changed by the time it makes it into print. There are two main reasons — the pressures of newspaper production and the weaknesses of most releases.

This is what happens to your release and what you can do to reduce the chances of mistakes and changes creeping in:

1. A reporter will write it up, possibly adding new information of his own. *Tip*: provide all the information the reporter needs. Don't leave loose ends in the story. Be available to provide more information or explanation.

2. The story will be passed to a sub-editor who will take a look at it and may rewrite it bringing out a new aspect. *Tip*: Give your story a clear theme or 'angle'. If it already has a good angle, the sub will be less tempted to find another.

3. On a national newspaper, the story will be passed to a page sub-editor, generally working on the 'back-bench' where executive decisions about what goes into the paper and how it is displayed are made. At this stage, the presentation and prominence of the story will be decided. *Tip*: not much you can do here, but a strong story will win more space.

4. Finally, the story may pass through a 'stone sub', the journalist who makes last minute cuts to ensure that a story fits into the space allotted for it. This is where information can be cut out at the last minute in order to make the story fit the space available. *Tip*: put the most important information at the top of the story. Use your facts in descending order of importance — then the least important will be cut.

Because your story may pass through all these stages, it needs to start off strong in theme, robust in structure, clear in expression and finite in detail if it is to survive the course.

Question and answer

Question: In the past, I've issued press releases which get into the paper in a completely garbled way. Why is this?

Answer: Quite possibly, the main point of the story wasn't clear. Could everything you wrote be understood by a non-expert? Make sure what you write is simply expressed, fully explained and unambiguous.

THE NEED FOR POSITIVE ACTION

'Why is it our competitors always seem to be in the press more than we are?' The question is often asked by managing directors miffed at another publicity coup by a hated rival. The sad fact is that the managing director's company is probably no less intrinsically newsworthy than his rival's. The difference is that the rival is taking positive action to publicise its newsworthy aspects to the press.

This means that a company that wants to see itself in the press needs to start off by taking some policy decisions at a high level. In a small to medium-sized company, the managing director will almost certainly be involved in the decisions. In medium-sized companies, the marketing or sales director might lead the press relations push. In larger companies there may even be a purpose-built press relations department.

Whichever is the case, whoever is in charge of deciding policy must recognise that the idea that press relations is somehow 'free' publicity is a myth. Certainly, your company will not pay for the coverage it will receive in the press in the way it would pay for advertising space. Yet gathering, preparing and disseminating news stories takes time and costs money. So if you want to develop a press relations programme you need to answer the questions in the next checklist even before you begin.

Checklist

Questions to answer before starting a press relations campaign.

1. Who will take decisions about the issues to be publicised?

2. Who will do the work of gathering information and writing the press releases?

3.　Who will approve the press releases for issue?

4.　What budget will be allocated for the task?

5.　How will that budget be broken down between staff time and sundry expenses?

6.　Will we use an outside public relations agency or freelance writer to write the releases?

7.　What do we realistically expect to achieve from our press relations campaign?

When, and only when, you have answered these questions are you ready to embark on your press relations campaign.

Action point: suggested answer
Your scores:
  1 - 5　shouldn't have sent the release;
  6 - 10　the wrong story in the wrong place;
11 - 15　needed a complete rewrite;
16 - 20　could have been sharpened up;
21 - 25　it must have hit the headlines.

Final thought: piggy in the middle
Are you thinking of taking on the job of press officer for the first time? Make sure you're doing it for the right reasons. Dealing with the media — newspapers and television — might sound more interesting than your present work, even glamorous. But it can have just as many gutty moments as any other job. Sometimes, you'll find yourself piggy in the middle — caught between avaricious journalists who want to know more and senior managers who want to reveal little. You'll need to be tough, shrewd and calm. Make sure you measure up before you take on the job.

2
Sitting on a Story

'If you have to tell them who you are, you aren't anybody.' — said by Gregory Peck in a restaurant when nobody recognised him.

But, then, to disagree with Mr Peck, if you don't tell them who you are they will never ever know. And the point about press relations is to let them know who you are, what you do, why you do it, and the benefits they (whoever 'they' are) can gain from it.

However, the problem with many organisations is to persuade the managers in it that it is worth starting a press relations campaign. It will never be possible to mount a successful press relations campaign in an organisation if the management does not believe press relations is worthwhile.

OVERCOMING OBJECTIONS TO PRESS RELATIONS

Here are some typical objections to press relations — and the answers to them.

Objection 1: It's a waste of managers' time
Answer: Properly managed press relations need not take up much management time and it can be time well spent. What can be more important than making sure customers, investors, employees and other key groups understand what your organisation is really about?

Objection 2: It costs too much
Answer: Certainly some large companies spend a fortune on wide-ranging public relations campaigns (which include many other activities than press relations). And some public relations consultants charge fancy fees for little result. But at the end of this book you will be able to generate your own highly effective press releases — at an annual cost which is less than the price of a glossy sales brochure.

Objection 3: The media wouldn't be interested in us

Answer: Journalists of the old-school have an adage — behind every front-door there is a good story. That applies to companies and non-profit making organisations as much as to private houses. Often what you find common-place, outsiders will find fascinating.

Objection 4: The media distorts everything anyway

Answer: Not so. Often inaccuracies or 'distortions' in the media occur because journalists do not know the true facts — they haven't been able to find them. There are some incidents of 'sensationalism' in the national tabloid press, but generally most journalists toil assiduously to find the truth and print it accurately.

Objection 5: We haven't the skills to run a press relations campaign

Answer: Possibly. But like other management activities, the skills can be acquired by training and practice. At the end of this book, you should be able to mount a creditable press relations campaign.

Action point

Which managers in your organisation could be hostile to press relations? Have you found out the basis of their objections? Make that a priority. Then use the ideas above to overcome them.

HOW TO TAP YOUR NEWS POTENTIAL

All organisations have news that someone, somewhere wants to hear about. To succeed, you need to do four things:

● *Find* the story.

● Decide *who* will be interested in it — the audience.

● Discover the best *channels* (newspapers, magazines and broadcast programmes) to reach the audience.

● *Present* the story in a way that will encourage the channels to use it.

We will be looking at the last three points in later chapters. The first step is to identify potential stories, the next step to decide how best to use them. Where do you start in looking for stories in your organisation? A good point is to begin with the four Ps: People, Products, Places, Profits.

People
The people in your organisation are news. There could be a news story when somebody:

- joins the company
- retires
- is promoted or takes on a new post
- is elected to a professional body
- wins an award
- makes a speech at a business conference
- wins a big order
- invents a new product
- takes part in a charity activity.

Products
Products are newsworthy, too. There could be a story when:

- a new product is launched
- an old product is revamped
- another company's product is acquired
- the product takes a leading market share
- the product is bought by a well-known organisation
- the product is used by a famous person
- the product is exported
- the 1,000th/1 millionth is sold
- the product is praised by independent commentators
- new technology is used
- a fresh design is introduced
- new material is used
- new packaging is introduced.

Places
This is a shorthand way for dealing with stories that arise from the locations at which your business takes place. There could be a places story when:

- new offices/factory are opened
- out-of-date offices/factory are closed
- offices/factory are modernised

- company is relocated
- new branches/shops are opened
- new distributors are opened in specific areas
- a new product has a special regional connotation.

Profits

This category of story covers most of the financial aspects of the company. All companies must lodge copies of their financial results with Companies House, where anybody can look at them for a fee. It is true that public companies have, by law, to provide more information than private companies, but both can create news stories based on their financial successes. There could be a story in this category when:

- annual financial results are announced
- quarterly/half yearly results are announced
- new investors take a stake in the company
- the company cuts prices
- the company funds a charitable or community project
- the company announces an investment programme.

The lists above are certainly not exhaustive, but they provide a starting point for your news hunt. They should start you thinking about the stories you can generate in your organisation.

Question and answer

Question: What if we're a small organisation? Will we still be able to find these stories?

Answer: Yes. Many of the categories will still be relevant but you may have a lower volume of stories. However, by adopting a pro-active press relations campaign and making the most of the stories you've got, you can make your company seem bigger than it is.

Action point

How could the story ideas in the lists above be used in your organisation? Go through the lists and make notes on specific stories that you might be able to use in the next three months.

PUTTING THE BASICS IN PLACE

One reason why many companies never get their press relations programmes off the ground is that they do not appoint one person with the authority to drive the programme.

Alternatively, the boss appoints somebody who is overloaded with so much other work, he or she doesn't have time to tackle press relations. Press relations can be rewarding work and deliver big benefits to the company, but it is time consuming. If your press relations campaign is to succeed you need the basics in place before you start.

As usual, the buck stops at the top person's desk. It is the responsibility of the managing director, or in larger companies the marketing/sales director, to ensure that one individual has the time and resources to run the press relations campaign. If the job of press relations is combined with other marketing activities — quite reasonable in smaller companies — the person responsible should clearly understand how much of his or her time is to be devoted to press relations.

Two resources the press officer needs

There are two other 'resources' the press relations manager will need. These are **authority** and a **budget**.

Authority

One reason why press relations campaigns stumble is that senior managers are not prepared to cooperate fully with the person running the campaign. Often the press officer will be lower down the pecking order than the senior managers. They might regard the campaign as a waste of time, a nuisance or a distraction from more important tasks. We have seen earlier in this chapter how to deal with some of these objections.

But firmer action is needed. The managing director needs to make it clear to all other senior managers that the press relations campaign is important in achieving the company's business objectives, and that they should cooperate fully with the person putting it into practice. Circulating a memo similar to the one in Figure 1 (page 30) deals with the matter.

Budget

Press relations is sometimes described as 'free' publicity. Don't believe it. Certainly, you do not pay for it, as you would advertising. But it costs money to run an effective press relations campaign. You will need to set aside a budget to ensure that the campaign is properly funded. Just how large that budget is depends on the size of the campaign and the nature of your company. The budget could contain all or some of the following items in this checklist:

Staff time   _____
Stationery   _____

MEMORANDUM

From: managing director (or marketing director)
To: heads of departments/other senior managers

The board has decided that in order to achieve our corporate objectives, we should adopt a higher profile in the media. To this end, we are launching a press relations campaign which will result in us featuring in more newspaper and magazine articles and, possibly on TV and radio.

I have appointed Hilda Headline of the marketing department as our press officer to manage this activity. She will combine it with her other marketing duties.

In order to ensure the success of the campaign, Hilda will need a steady flow of news stories from all departments. She will be contacting all heads of departments in the next few days with some more detailed information about how the press relations campaign will be conducted.

I want to make it clear she does this with the board's and my full approval. Within reason, you should make time to deal with her requests and provide the information she will need to perform her tasks successfully.

The press relations campaign is important in helping us to achieve our corporate objectives in the coming year and I know I can count on your enthusiastic cooperation.

Fig. 1. A memorandum to win the hearts and minds of your staff.

Postage   _____
Telephone   _____
Printing/photocopying (of press releases)   _____
Photography   _____
Travelling   _____
Hospitality (for entertaining journalists)   _____
Other office overheads.   _____

Question and answer

Question: My organisation is sympathetic to the idea of a press relations campaign, but some managers say we can't afford it. Is there anything we can do?

Answer: Although press relations does cost money, it is not expensive in relation to other marketing expenditures. Suggest to your colleagues that you take a look at the total marketing budget to see if some of it could more effectively be spent on press relations.

GETTING THE FACTS

So far, so good. You have got the resources you need, courtesy of a generous managing director. Now you need to find news stories in your organisation to write about. The first thing you need to know is that although you may occasionally stumble across a great story, most news is discovered as the result of hard work.

The next thing to know is that you will not find the good stories you need without the cooperation of other people in your organisation. Moreover, although some people like the idea of personal publicity and are, therefore, quite willing to cooperate in pulling together the facts for a press release, in other cases people may be less willing to help. Busy managers, for example, might believe their time is better spent on other activities.

Bearing these facts in mind, what personal qualities will you need as a successful press officer? A *Sunday Times* writer once said the qualities needed by a journalist were 'a little literary ability, a plausible manner and rat-like cunning.' Those might be quite suitable for a national paper newshound, but are not quite right for the company or organisation press officer. More appropriate qualities are summarised in the next checklist.

Checklist: qualities needed by a press officer
● An enquiring mind
● Persistence
● Ability to 'read' people

- Tact
- Foresight
- Mastery of detail
- Ability to work accurately
- Clear, grammatical English
- Sense of urgency
- Desire to communicate.

Action point
Who do you plan to appoint as your press officer? Test him/her against the qualities in the checklist. Mark each quality in a scale of one to five, where one equals hopeless and five equals excellent. Total the marks (maximum 50). Then turn to the end of the chapter for an assessment.

CREATING YOUR OWN NEWS GATHERING SYSTEM

If you are to feed the media with a regular stream of interesting press releases, you need to create a news gathering system within your organisation. This could be quite elaborate in a large organisation with thousands of employees, but much simpler in a smaller organisation. The essential elements of an organisation-wide news gathering system are these.

The press officer
This is the person who is responsible for managing the press relations campaign and making sure that the campaign is linked to the organisation's overall objectives. The press officer will:

- find news stories
- turn them into press releases
- release them to relevant media
- act as a first point of contact for journalists
- monitor press coverage
- disseminate press coverage within the organisation
- report on the effects of press coverage to senior managers.

In some cases, usually in larger organisations, the press officer will report on a day-to-day basis to a more senior manager, often the marketing director. In other cases, the press officer will report to the managing director. The degree of autonomy given to the press officer varies widely from one organisation to another. Generally, it is wise to allow the press officer wide autonomy over the operational aspects of his or her job, but provide a level of senior management control over the policy aspects, such as the kind of press releases issued and the way the organisation is presented.

News contacts

These people play the role of what journalists call **stringers** — local reporters with their ear to the ground who feed in stories to the news desks of national and regional newspapers. In a small company, the press officer will often know about everything newsworthy that happens. That will not be possible in a larger company with several departments and branch offices.

In this case, the press officer should appoint a news contact in each branch. The news contact is responsible for keeping a weather eye open for potential press release stories and telling the press officer about them.

The press officer should brief each news contact on the kind of stories he or she is looking for. It is also important to maintain the enthusiasm of news contacts. One way to do this is to make sure they see the fruits of their efforts. The press officer should provide them with a regular collection of press cuttings, especially of stories which they initiated.

Action point

What news contacts will you need in your organisation? Make a list of the branches or departments where you feel you may need a news contact. Discuss with branch managers or departmental heads who the news contacts might be.

An approval system

Press relations needs to be properly managed, like any other business activity. One important element of news gathering and dissemination is an approval system. The organisation needs to lay down a policy for approving press releases.

Generally speaking, the following people need to be involved in this:

The press officer
To coordinate the process and advise on the newsworthiness and journalistic presentation of each story.

A senior manager
To ensure each press release fits in with the organisation's overall policies.

A manager
To be responsible for the business area dealt with in the release. He or she makes sure the release deals accurately with the subject.

Anyone quoted in the release
To make sure they are happy with the words quoted.

Figure 2 shows how these people inter-relate.

Nothing undermines corporate confidence in press relations more than press releases that are inaccurate, which give away information that should remain confidential, or which lead to embarrassing publicity. A properly managed approval system helps to avoid all these pitfalls.

Action point

When do you plan to set up an approval system in your organisation? Will the managers involved clearly understand what their responsibilities are?

WHERE TO FIND INFORMATION FOR PRESS RELEASES

Good, reliable information is the raw material of a press release. That means you need to give particular attention to getting the information for each release. Depending on the organisation, there can be several sources of information for potential press releases.

Talking to people

By far the most effective way. Regular informal contact with a wide range of people in your organisation will keep you in touch with what is going on. You may find that some people become regular sources of story ideas. For example, the marketing manager can provide regular stories about products, the personnel manager about newsworthy new appointments. In cases like these, it is probably worthwhile setting up a regular review meeting so that you can collect the information in a structured way. When you have identified a possible story idea, you will need to interview the people concerned. Effective techniques for doing that are described in the next section.

Reports

Most organisations churn out reports on different aspects of their work and products. Most reports will be for internal consumption and of no interest to outsiders. But the odd one will contain information you can rework into an interesting press release.

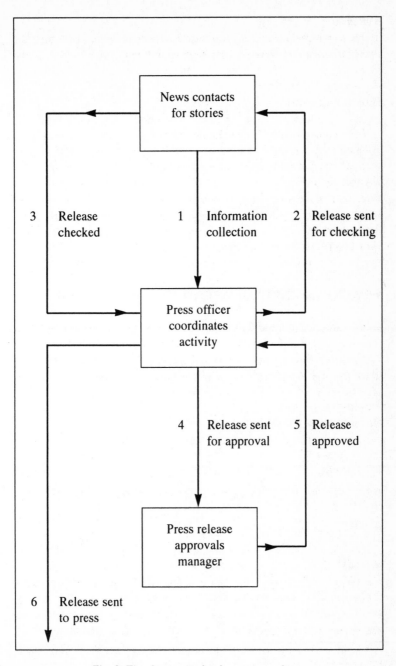

Fig. 2. The six steps to issuing a press release.

Minutes of meetings

These report decisions taken and future courses of action. Providing the decisions are not organisation-confidential they could be of interest to the media.

Internal literature

Such as product briefings, company newspapers, employee briefings. These frequently contain information that you can rework into a press release.

Action point

It is important that you identify potential sources of information for press releases in your organisation. Have you made sure you are on the circulation list for any relevant documents? Do you systematically review them for potential media stories?

HOW TO CONDUCT AN INTERVIEW

As we have seen, you discover most stories by talking to people. When you have found a possible story, you need to get the most newsworthy information about it. You do that best by interviewing those people who know about it. As a press release writer, you will find that conducting an effective interview falls into three main phases.

Before the interview

To begin with, you need to identify the following information about your interviewee:

● His/her name (including its correct spelling and pronunciation).

● Title and position in the organisation.

● His/her relationship to the story idea you have identified. (For example, is he the product manager in charge of releasing the new product, is he a user of the product? etc.)

Three types of interview

Next, you need to decide what kind of interview you are going to conduct. It could be:

Face to face
This is best when you need to conduct a reasonably lengthy interview. In journalistic terms, this means more than about 30-45 minutes. It is also best when the subject matter is technical and you may need to review documents, such as diagrams or manuals, during the interview. Another benefit of conducting a face to face interview is that it will sometimes help you to identify possible pictures to accompany the story. You will often find that people 'open up' more in face to face interviews, so you have a better chance of getting more detail in the story.

Telephone
This is best when you only need to conduct a short interview and the interviewee is some distance away. (If they're in your office, interview them face to face.) One example is the interview for a 'new appointment' release, where the amount of information you need is fairly small and you don't need to talk on the phone for more than 10 minutes or so. Another benefit is that busy people are sometimes more willing to fit in a telephone interview than schedule another meeting.

Correspondence
This is not usually desirable, but in a few cases may be unavoidable. Sometimes you can only get the information you need by exchanging letters, faxes, or e-mails with your interviewee. In a case where the information you need to get is very technical, this method can actually be beneficial. But the danger of this approach for most news stories is that the lack of personal contact can mean that you miss out on facts that could be used to enrich the story and which somehow never seem to get mentioned in written briefings.

Problem and remedy
Problem: What happens if the person I need to get the information from is not keen on being interviewed?
   Remedy: He may be worried that you will take up too much of his time or that your questions will reveal gaps in his knowledge. Tackle the twin problem by making it clear how much time you will need (often not that much). Deal with the knowledge gap by providing an outline of the ground you want to cover during the interview. Stress that the interview will be completely informal.

Focus on the interview subject
Before the interview, you should establish in your own mind what

information you want to get out of it. One way of clarifying this is to focus on five favourite words of journalists:

Who? _____

What? _____

When? _____

Where? _____

Why? _____

Any good news story centres around answering these questions. Sometimes it also includes answers to the question 'how?'.

You need to come away from your interview with detailed information about:

● What is happening.
● Who is doing it, and who will be affected by it.
● When it is happening.
● Where it is happening.
● Why and how it will be done.

Three steps in conducting an interview

If you have not interviewed anybody before for a press release or article, you may be worried about what to do. There is no need to be. You can approach the interview with more confidence if you go through three steps:

Understand your brief

Know why you are going to write a press release, and the kind of newspapers or magazines it will be aimed at. This will help you to understand the kind of information you need to collect during the interview.

Make contact with your interviewee

Find out his or her name and position within the organisation. Try to get some initial information to help you gauge his relationship to the news story you are going to write. Brief the person on what information you want, so that he or she has time to pull it together before the interview. Finally fix a firm time for the interview (even if it is going to be over the telephone) and a place, if appropriate. In general, go to the person. Tell the interviewee how long you think you will need.

NOTES FOR AN INTERVIEW: 1

Branch name? _____

Address of branch? _____

How large? _____

  — staff _____

  — square feet _____

  — turnover _____

  — investment _____

When opening? _____

  — any ceremony? _____

What territory covered by new
branch? _____

  — how does this impact on
existing branches? _____

Any special activities at
branch? _____

Why this branch now? _____

Name of manager _____

Fig. 3. Notes for an interview about a new branch opening.

NOTES FOR AN INTERVIEW: 2

Name of product? _____

When launched? _____

New or upgrade? _____

What does it do? _____

— what's new here? _____

— any major innovation? _____

— anything not done before? _____

How is it positioned in market? _____

— where does it differ from
competitors? _____

Who will main user be? _____

— any already? _____

How large estimated market? _____

— any research here? _____

What about distribution
channels? _____

— special offers? _____

— maintenance and support? _____

— wholesale and retail price? _____

Marketing, advertising and
promotion? _____

Who is heading the new
product? _____

Technical detail for background (if appropriate) _____

Fig. 4. Notes for an interview about a new product launch.

Think through the structure of your interview
If you are to get the information you need, you should help the interviewee give it to you. If you conduct a haphazard interview, it is likely your interviewee will forget to give you vital facts, or may overlook useful detail that would bring your press release to life. So think through how you will conduct the interview.

This could mean writing down an interview plan, possibly as a series of one or two word notes on the topics you want to cover. You might want to write down a few key questions, but it is a mistake to try to write down all the questions. Interviews have a habit of taking off in an unexpected direction and you want to retain the flexibility to react to that.

Figures 3 and 4 show some simple notes that you might prepare for two typical stories, one dealing with the opening of a new branch, the other with the announcement of a new product.

Action point
To test your understanding of interview structure, draw up some simple notes for an interview with a new branch manager. You will issue a press release about the manager's new appointment. Use the who, what, when, where, why formula. Don't forget that the 'how' often provides the detail a specialist publication will need. Check your version with the suggestion at the end of this chapter.

Note-taking or tape recording?
Before the interview starts, you should decide whether you are going to make notes or record the interview. There are pros and cons to both approaches.

Note-taking
First, you need a good note-taking ability — either shorthand or speed-writing. Writing everything down laboriously in longhand won't do. It will take too long and you will not look very professional to your interviewee.

One trick needed with note-taking is the ability to be scribbling away while asking your next question. This is a skill that is acquired with practice.

Note-taking is an efficient way of recording an interview if you do it efficiently — and can read your notes afterwards. On the other hand, an unskilled note-taker may miss vital detail, especially in an interview on a complex or technical subject. Another advantage of note-taking is that you can use notes to write your story as soon as you get back to the office (indeed, it is advisable to do so as soon as you get back) and don't have the often tedious task of listening to and transcribing a tape.

Recording

A few years ago, most interviewees would have raised an eyebrow when a journalist brought out a tape-recorder. Now the machines are commonplace (you see journalists using them on the TV news every night). Additionally, with miniaturisation, the machines have become so small it is arguable they are less intrusive in an interview than note-taking.

There are many advantages in recording an interview. You can concentrate all your attention on your interviewee without the distraction of note-taking. You record every word spoken. You can listen to the interview again and again, valuable in complex passages where you may not have grasped the full meaning the first time around. You have a definitive record of what was said over which there can be no dispute (although this is not too important when you will be gaining approval for your press release text).

However, there are several disadvantages. You have to transcribe those parts of the tape you need after the interview and that can take time. In any interview, there will be a lot of things said that are not strictly relevant, and you must listen to those again as the tape is played. There is a remote danger of a fault which means the recording equipment doesn't work. The worst case is where it seems to have worked, but the tape turns out to be blank.

Finally, recording machines pick up background noise, which in some cases can block out important parts of the interview. That may mean you may have to request a window or door to the outer office is closed before an interview can begin.

During the interview

An interview is a kind of one-sided conversation in which you ask most of the questions and your interlocutor provides most of the answers. Like any conversation, the kind of interview you will hold in order to gain information for a press release should be conducted in polite, friendly conversational tones. Forget the image of Jeremy Paxman grilling some hapless politician. You are not in the same business as a television interviewer. And, indeed, the styles of television and press interviews are completely different.

Your purpose is to get the information you need to meet your brief. So you should conduct the interview in a way that helps your interviewee provide it. Look at your interview notes shortly before the interview and by all means have your interview structure in front of you during the meeting.

Take your interviewee through the main points you want to cover in a logical way. Give enough time to each topic to ensure that you have fully understood what you have been told. Do not be afraid to ask the same question in different words if you feel your interviewee has not provided quite the information you want the first time around.

If your interviewee answers a question too briefly, don't be afraid to ask for more detail. If he or she goes on for too long, politely point out that the press release will be comparatively short and you need information on just a few key areas. Do not be afraid to ask your interviewee to explain any concept you don't understand or to spell key names.

Know when to bring the interview to a close. Glance back over your interview structure, and satisfy yourself that you have covered all the points in it — especially the five Ws. Then close the interview with words such as: 'Thank you for sparing the time to see me today. I think I've asked all the questions I wanted, is there anything else you would like to add?' This gives your interviewee the chance to touch on a topic you might not have thought to ask about. You will be surprised how often it happens. So don't be afraid to ask supplementary questions about it if you need to.

Checklist: Ten tips for interviews

- Prepare in advance.
- Arrive on time.
- Inspire confidence.
- Know what you want from the interview.
- Check facts, especially spelling, numbers, etc.
- Tease out interesting detail.
- Say when you don't understand something.
- Be politely persistent in getting the facts you need.
- Check back afterwards for any facts you missed.
- Thank the interviewee for his or her help — you may need it again.

After the interview

When you get back to the office, write up your story as soon as you conveniently can. In this way, the facts of the story are still fresh in your mind. So is your enthusiasm for the story. There is nothing worse than putting off writing a story you feel may be difficult to get down on paper. As the days roll by, the thought of writing the story becomes more daunting — and you forget more about it.

When writing your story, don't be afraid to check back with your interviewee if there is any point you don't understand or a fact which is not clear. There is a well-worn journalists' maxim which is useful none-theless: if in doubt, leave it out. As you will not want to leave out vital facts you must check them.

Action point
Are you confident about your interviewing skills? If not, run a role playing exercise with the assistance of two helpful and candid colleagues. Choose a subject for a mock interview and interview colleague A. Afterwards, ask colleague B for comments. Then reverse the process and ask colleague A for comments on your interview with colleague B.

Check your scores (page 32)
Qualities needed by a press officer. Assessment guidelines.

  0 - 9 don't let them near the job.

10 - 19 find someone else if you can.

20 - 29 a possible choice but will need some help to find his or her feet.

30 - 39 a good choice.

40 - 50 this person ought to be editing a national newspaper (or doing your job).

Understanding interview structure
See page 41. Your interview could look something like this:

Who:	name of manager
	age
	marital status
	children
	previous career details
What:	nature of appointment
	formal title
Where:	which branch
When:	date he or she takes up appointment
Why:	reason for new branch manager
	ie did previous manager move, retire, etc.
Other:	quote from new manager on what he or she hopes to achieve.

3
Finding the Target

'I shot an arrow into the air, It fell to earth, I knew not where.'

H W Longfellow.

THE NEED FOR GOOD TARGETING

When you launch a press relations campaign, you don't want to be like Longfellow's archer. Unfortunately, many (possibly even most) public relations folk spray out their press releases indiscriminately. Few take the trouble to find out whether the newspapers and magazines they bombard with material will be interested in it.

Does that matter? The answer is a resounding yes. There are three reasons why sending out press releases thither and yon will damage your long-term chances of gaining press coverage.

The irritant factor

By annoying journalists with irrelevant material, you may miss an opportunity to grab their attention when you do have something useful to contribute. Journalists become adept at recognising sources of useless as well as useful information.

Here is what journalist and author Keith Waterhouse said about the topic: 'Ninety five per cent of the handouts that reach me as a *Daily Mail* columnist don't even reach the scrunching stage. They glide unread and often unopened — you get to recognise the envelopes — straight from desk to bin.' Waterhouse isn't alone. One of journalists' biggest moans is being deluged with irrelevant press handouts.

The cash waste

Post a press release to 50 journalists once a fortnight and you run up an annual postage bill of £338 (at 1998 postage rates). Add in printing and stationery and costs rise to around £600 a year.

If three-quarters of those releases miss the target, you are wasting £450 a year, money that could be spent in other ways to make the press relations campaign work better.

The blurred focus

The more journalists you have on your mailing list for a particular release, the more you try to put something in that will grab their attention. Your release starts to lose its focus. Instead of appealing to everybody, it appeals to nobody.

There is only so much information that can be carefully packed into a focused press release. Know who you are aiming each release at and choose facts that will be of special interest to them.

Problem and remedy

Problem: Some of our managers think all we have to do is to send a press release to an editor and he will automatically print it. What can I do to persuade them it is not as easy as that?

Remedy: You need to make it clear that press coverage is not a right, but something you have to win. Your managers will know that they have to win sales on the merits of the product and the service your company provides. You should point out that press coverage is won on merit, too — the newsworthiness of the press releases you provide.

HOW TO IDENTIFY YOUR TARGET AUDIENCES

Even before you send out your first press release, you need to do some careful thinking. What is the point of sending out press releases? And who are you trying to reach?

Often the point of sending press releases is to tell customers and potential customers about your products or services. But there are other reasons. You might want investors to read about your company more often. You may want to be better understood by politicians and policy-makers. You may want your company to have a more caring image in its local community.

It is important to think through these and similar questions and decide who your **prime audiences** are. Who do you want to read about your company? Exactly what kind of people are you trying to reach? If you do not answer these questions before you start your press campaign, it will lack the focus it needs in order to serve your business plan.

But how do you decide what kind of people you most need to reach?

Let us take three examples.

● Comfiseat is a company making hand-built country-style furniture which it sells through specialist retailers all over Britain. It wants more people to know about the furniture it makes. Its existing customers usually live in up-market property. It also wants to increase the number of retailers selling its products. Clearly, it has dual objectives — to reach people who live in big houses (its potential customers) and retailers who run specialist furniture stores (its potential distribution channels).

● Office Efficiency is a computer software distributor that has just introduced an American developed package to the British market. The package, called Coordinator, helps managers fix meetings, record events, and monitor decisions that need to be taken or reviewed. Office Efficiency's customers will be middle-ranking managers in medium to large companies, many of whom will have specialist information technology knowledge. Its objective, therefore, is to gain press coverage that wins the attention of these people.

● Safehands Insurance is a nationally known company which runs a major office complex in a medium-sized town. Since the company first established itself there, other companies have sprung up on industrial estates around the town, making it more difficult for Safehands to attract the large number of clerical and administrative workers it needs from the local population. It needs to communicate more effectively with local people in order to persuade them that Safehands Insurance is an interesting and pleasant place to work.

The common theme running through these imaginary cases — and, of course, in real-life ones — is the need to use press coverage to help solve real business problems. In each case, our companies have asked themselves two questions:

● What business problem do we need to solve?

● Which people do we need to reach to solve it?

Action point
Now ask yourself the same questions about your organisation.

1. What are the most pressing business problems you need to solve at the moment?

2. Have your senior managers discussed them recently?

3. Have they reached any kind of consensus view?

4. Has that view been communicated to other staff?

5. In particular, has any thought been given to how press relations could help solve the problems?

You need to raise all these questions and find the answers in your own organisation if you are to perform successfully as the press officer.

Focus produces better results

To help you identify the people you need to reach, think in terms of three groups:

● Users and potential users of your products and services.

● People and organisations who help you make and distribute the product.

● People and organisations who influence the business and economic climate in which you operate.

Figure 5 provides some more detail on the categories of people you might want to reach with your press relations campaign. Few organisations will want to reach all categories, but most will want to reach several.

Action point

Spend some time thinking about which people you want to reach. Work through the list in Figure 5. Which categories are relevant in your case? Can you be more precise about the people you need to reach in each category?

All this may seem rather dull work. You may ask: why are we doing this and not getting on with writing press releases? The answer is that if you do not know who you are writing the releases for, you will produce material that is unfocused. Because your press releases don't home in on the real-life business concerns of your target audiences, they will not provide them with anything useful and will not deliver any benefit to your organisation.

1. Our customers ☐

2. Rival's customers ☐

3. Possible users of our product ☐

4. Our management ☐

5. Our staff ☐

6. Our suppliers ☐

7. Dealers/distributors ☐

8. Retailers ☐

9. Government departments ☐

10. Members of Parliament ☐

11. Local councils ☐

12. European Union ☐

13. European Parliament ☐

14. Investors ☐

15. Educational bodies ☐

16. Special interest groups ☐

Fig. 5. Target audiences for a press relations campaign.

Problem and remedy

Problem: Our managing director wants to put out press releases just so that he can see his name in the paper. Should I go along with him?

Remedy: Not if you can avoid it. Point out to him that releases issued with no other purpose than to gain self-serving publicity for the people mentioned in them rarely generate much coverage. Show him that he is much more likely to gain coverage if he allows you to issue releases that provide some real news value to the publications which receive them.

DRAWING UP YOUR OWN COMPANY PRESS LIST

Once you have decided on the people you need to reach, the next step is to find out about the publications which they read. Britain probably has one of the most comprehensive ranges of newspapers and magazines in the world.

In some cases it will be obvious which newspapers and magazines are the favourite reading matter of your target audiences. After all, some publications advertise their audience in their title. Flip through a media directory and you will find publications as diverse as *Sea Angler*, *Senior Nurse*, *Airline Business*, *Driver Magazine* and *Table Tennis News*. With publications that announce their interests so conveniently, finding targets is not too hard.

Similarly, if you are trying to reach people in a specific town, the local evening and weekly papers will be important. In the case of specific business audiences, there is a vast choice of specialist journals, ranging from accountancy to zoology, which you could target for your press release.

But in other cases it may not be so clear which are the best publications to reach your target audiences. In these cases, you will need to do some research. For example, if you are trying to reach new potential customers, ask existing customers what publications they read. You could run a postal or telephone survey of them and give them an incentive to take part by putting all completed survey forms into a prize draw.

If you are moving into new business areas, seek help from other companies already operating in the area. Perhaps you have suppliers who are active in the area and might be willing to provide some advice about the most read publications.

As you conduct your research, you will begin to build up a picture of the newspapers and magazines read by the people you most need to reach. The next step is to find out more information about these publications.

Where to find out about newspapers and magazines

Even if you know about the main newspapers and magazines operating in your market, you will probably still need some more detailed information about them. For example, you will need information about:

- Address
- Phone number
- Editor's name
- Names of certain specialist correspondents and writers.

Such information is available from a number of media directories. The main directories are:

PIMS UK Media Directory
Address: PIMS House, Mildmay Avenue, London N1 4RS. Tel: (0171) 226 1000.

- Contents: Lists of publications grouped in different categories. Names of editors for all publications. For national and regional newspapers, names of specialist correspondents. Lists of contacts on news and feature programmes on radio and TV. Lists of specialist freelance journalists covering areas such as agriculture, computers and medicine.

PIMS also publishes *PIMS Media Townlist* which identifies media in 1,100 towns and provides editorial contacts for local press, TV and radio. Other publications: media directories for Europe and the United States.

PR Planner
Address: Media Information Ltd, Chess House, Germain Street, Chesham, Bucks HP5 1SJ. Tel: (01494) 797260.

- Contents: Two volumes covering the UK and Europe. Similar listings to Pims with names of editors and special correspondents. Also covers radio and TV stations.

Editors
Address: Media Information Ltd, Chess House, Germain Street, Chesham, Bucks HP5 1SJ. Tel: (01494) 797260.

- Contents: Very comprehensive listings of newspapers and magazines and the journalists who work for them. Published in six volumes. Also contains details of forthcoming editorial features.

Two-Ten Media Directory
Address: Two-Ten Communications, Communications House, 210 Old Street, London EC1V 9UN. Tel: (0171) 490 8111.

● Contents: A bi-monthly directory of editorial media contacts. Also town-by-town listings and European Media Directory.

Willings Press Guide
Address: Hollis Directories, Harlequin House, 7 High Street, Teddington, Middx TW11 8EL. Tel: (0181) 977 7711.

● Contents: Contains lists of magazines and newspapers in Britain and overseas countries. Less detail than some of the other directories, but broader international coverage. Updated annually.

Benn's Media Directory
Address: Miller Freeman Ltd, Riverbank House, Angel Lane, Tonbridge, Kent TN9 1SE. Tel: (01732) 362666. Published in two volumes — UK and overseas. The UK volume lists newspapers and magazines, the former by town, the latter by subject. The overseas volume is one of the most comprehensive views of the international press around, listing 32,000 publications in 197 countries.

Media packs
By using these reference books, you should be able to draw up a reasonably accurate press list. But you may want to get more detailed information about some of the titles on your target list. If you need more information, there is a further way to obtain it.

Almost all newspapers and magazines produce **media packs** which describe editorial policy and advertising opportunities. Most media packs also provide a detailed breakdown of the publication's circulation. This information can help you decide whether the magazine or newspaper in question reaches your target audience. You can obtain a media pack by telephoning the publication's advertising department.

BUILDING A PUBLICATION PROFILE

How can you make sure your press releases stand out from the bulk that slide straight into the bin? As we have seen, a most effective way is to make sure that they are precisely targeted. There is a simple test of whether you are properly targeting your releases. Before you send each release, you should ask yourself whether the publication you are sending it to is reasonably likely to be interested in it.

The way to do this is to build a publication profile of each of the newspapers and magazines on your press list. In order to build a workable publication profile you need:

● at least three back numbers of each publication on the list
● two card index boxes
● supply of index cards.

The publication box

In the first card index box you create a profile card for each publication on your list. The first section of each card should contain the following information:

● name of publication
● address
● telephone number
● fax number
● name of editor
● names and titles of any journalists with whom you expect to be dealing (cookery, motoring, fashion, gardening correspondents, etc).
● E-mail address.

The second section of each card should contain an analysis of the kinds of stories the publication seems to be interested in and which you feel you might be able to make a contribution to. For example, does the publication write about new products? Does it carry comment from industry spokespeople? Does it have a financial page?

In the case of national and regional daily newspapers, the range of coverage will be extremely wide, but you will be able to focus on those parts of the publication likely to be interested in the news you have to offer. In the case of local newspapers and magazines, the range of coverage will be more focused.

The purpose of this exercise is to ensure that you only send relevant press releases to each publication, so you need to look at each newspaper and magazine and see which kinds of stories it carries. The checklist below shows some of the common types, but the range can be so large the list is not exhaustive.

Checklist: Analysing the contents of target publications
- home news
- international news
- financial news
- sports news
- diary column
- new appointments
- product news
- forthcoming events
- book reviews
- theatre/concert reviews
- personality profiles
- contributed feature articles
- case studies
- surveys
- new product literature
- women's page
- children's page/column
- medical page/column
- property
- gardening
- motoring
- small business column
- information technology
- product reviews
- agriculture
- music
- shopping
- personal finance
- cookery
- hobbies
- holidays
- travel

On each card you should list those kinds of stories carried. You should note other information about whether the publication accepts contributed photographs (colour or black and white), diagrams or other artwork.

On the back of each card, you can record notes about any contacts you have with journalists on the publication.

Perhaps a journalist on one paper receives a press release from you and calls for further information. He might mention that he is particularly interested in stories about a certain topic. This is the kind of information worth noting for future reference.

As you create your publication box file, each card in box 1 should look something like the sample in Figure 6 (page 56).

The story target box

The publication box file grows into a mine of information. It becomes an invaluable source of reference about targets for particular types of stories and photographs, as well as the hobby-horses of individual journalists. Yet if you have a large number of publications you are trying to reach, it can be unwieldy. You might need quick answers to questions like:

● Which newspapers accept new appointment photographs?
● Which women's magazines accept contributed recipes?
● What regional newspapers run book review pages?
● Which magazines test drive cars?
● What consumer magazines carry a regular property column?
● Which local newspapers in Greater London review restaurants?

The story target box is an ideal way to store this information so you have it readily to hand. You want a quick reference to those publications that accept colour product photos? You can find it quickly in your story target box, along with the answers to dozens of other enquiries. Even more, you have a system that directs your energies towards sending information to editors that they really want to receive. And that can only make your press relations more successful.

Problem and remedy

Problem: Producing these files sounds like a lot of work. I don't think I've got time to do it.

Remedy: You haven't got time not to do it. These files will eventually save you hours of effort and make sure your press relations activity is well directed. Besides, don't think you have to set up the whole files at once. The files will grow naturally as your press relations campaign develops. A further benefit: when you hand over the press relations responsibility to somebody else, all the information you have accumulated is handed on too.

Now computerise it

With your two boxes you have created a cross-indexed system that will enable you to target your press releases with laser beam precision. Trouble

EVENING GRAPHIC

26 News Street, Papertown, Prints. PT6 8DW

Tel: (01799) 670021

Fax: (01799) 670022

Editor: Fred Spike

Business reporter: Jim Standfirst

- JS wants stories on local companies that win big new contracts.

- Runs new appts column on Tuesdays

- Editor often praises companies who show concern for the local community

Fig. 6. What a publication box card might look like.

is, any manual system takes a lot of clerical effort to operate. If you are going into press relations only in a small way, the box system should serve you well.

If you are developing an intensive press relations campaign, you need to think about computerising your record system and the distribution of your releases. You have two main options:

1. Develop a record system on your own PC using any one of the numerous database packages readily available on the market. That is a good option if you are reasonably computer literate or have somebody in the organisation who is and who also has the time to set up and maintain the system for you.

2. The other option is to use one of the computerised bureau services run by press contact and distribution specialists.

Two services that could provide what you need are:

●   PIMS Computer Link, Pims House, Mildmay Avenue, London N1 4RS. Tel: (0171) 226 1000. With this system you use your own PC to gain access to PIMS' master database over the telephone lines, using a modem. You can view information on the media directories' database (see PIMS entry on page 51), print labels for press release distribution and maintain your own private lists.

●   Two-Ten Targeter, Communications House, 210 Old Street, London EC1V 9UN. Tel: (0171) 490 8111. This system works in a similar way to PIMS. You need an IBM-compatible PC from which you then access the PNA database across the telephone lines. The database carries details of 11,000 UK media and 27,000 named journalists. If you want to, you can send your press release and target journalists' list direct to PNA, using electronic mail. PNA will print the release and distribute it for you.

Action point
Have you estimated the volume of press releases you will be issuing? How often will you be issuing them? Do you have the clerical resources to cope? You need to plan the logistics of printing and issuing your releases.

4
Stories that Score

'Sixty horses wedged in a chimney. The story to fit this sensational headline has not yet turned up.' — J. B. Morton, journalist, also known as 'Beachcomber'.

However, we can be quite certain that if the story did turn up it would be the front page lead in every national newspaper. You are unlikely to be able to write a press release to fit that headline, either. So you must now turn your attention to the kinds of stories that you can produce and the ones that might interest editors.

FINDING OUT ABOUT NEWS VALUES

One problem facing the press officer is that a story which makes one newspaper's column inches proves to be another's bin liner. That is most noticeable with the national press, but it is also true of the approach of regional newspapers and even, sometimes, with trade papers covering the same industry area.

To get some idea of the problem, look at this list of the front page lead stories from the national press one morning:

● *Times:* Bomb blast at Sarajevo funeral

● *Daily Mail:* Hospital row over 'killer bug' at children's hospital

● *Daily Telegraph:* Bomb blast at Sarajevo funeral

● *The Sun:* Jail prisoner receives visits from 'kinky beauty'

● *Daily Mirror:* Hospital row over 'killer bug' at children's hospital

● *Daily Express:* Judge pleads to jail teenage torturer

● *Guardian:* Pressure for UN intervention in Bosnia mounts

- *Today:* Paroled sex criminal jailed after another attack

- *Independent:* Bomb blast at Sarajevo funeral

- *Financial Times:* Two banks to be sued for £490m.

Although there is some unanimity among the 'quality' press about the main news of the day, there is little among the tabloids, although two papers lead with the 'killer bug' story. Although none of these stories, and many of the others contained in the national press, contains any input from press releases, they can teach some useful lessons to press release writers.

News values differ from one paper to another
News values are best defined as the importance which the paper's editorial team attaches to different types of story. Even newspapers seemingly appealing to the same kind of market will have different news values.

Two examples from the national press illustrate the point:

- The *Daily Mirror* gives more coverage to stories about the National Health Service than *The Sun*.

- *The Independent* gives less coverage to stories about the Royal Family than the *Daily Telegraph*.

Sometimes newspapers take up a special campaign which can run on intermittently for years. For example, the *Daily Mail* takes a pride in exposing rogues in the timeshare holiday home business.

While you might expect these differences in news values in national newspapers, you might be surprised to find they also exist in the trade and technical press. One reason for this is that a publication's news values are one way in which it can differentiate itself from the competition.

What does all this mean to you as a press release writer? You could choose to ignore it. But if you want to gain an edge over your rivals, the more you understand about the news values of the publications to which you send your releases, and the more you try to tailor your stories to reflect those news values, the more you will succeed in getting them published.

Ways to find out about news values
There is no magic formula. You find out about the news values by reading the publications regularly and closely studying the kind of stories they run and the way they treat those stories. Even so, there are three points that may help you.

Look out for 'running stories'

Is there a story that is running from one issue to another? For example, the local council might be planning to build a new industrial estate on the outskirts of town. Local business is in favour, but residents' groups are against. The paper will carry new developments in the story from week to week. If you have something to say about the issue, you can plug your organisation into the debate and win helpful column inches.

Understand the point of view

What point of view does the publication take about different topics? For example, the *Today* newspaper took a strongly 'green' line on news stories for a period of time. If a story had a green angle, the paper played it up. And it went out of its way to look for good green stories which other papers hadn't run. If you understand the point of view of the publications you are trying to reach, you may be able to tailor your press material to accommodate it and, thus, stand more chance of getting it into print.

Watch for particular journalists' hobby-horses

Individual journalists, especially specialist correspondents covering particular industries or topics, often have their own hobby-horses, subjects which they take a special interest in or enjoy covering. If you have a story which seems to fit in with what such a journalist is writing about, then you could win coverage by angling your story specifically at him or her.

Problem and remedy

Problem: If a particular newspaper is interested in a subject, but not sympathetic to our point of view, should we send them our releases or not?

    Remedy: Yes, certainly send news of your activities. To some extent hostility is fuelled by ignorance. You will not make them more sympathetic to your point of view by cutting them off from information about your activities.

A QUESTION OF STYLE

Next you need to look more closely at the way the publications on your target list treat the stories they publish. For example, does the publication provide objective news coverage, or is the coverage strongly opinionated by the reporters and the policy of the publication? Does the publication take the subjects you are concerned with seriously or does it marginalise or, even worse, trivialise the issues?

    Then, again, what kind of style does the publication use? Is it a literate style, as used in the 'quality' press or a more popular style based on a limited vocabulary and short sentences with no subordinate clauses? What about such basic issues as the length of the stories and the amount of detail they contain?

Finally, what about issues such as the way material is laid out and illustrated? Does the publication use photographs (colour or black and white), cartoons, diagrams or technical drawings? Would you stand more chance of winning column inches if you provided some illustrative matter with the release?

You need to consider all these issues in planning for your press relations campaign. The basic message is this: the more you can understand about the publications you are sending your press releases to, and the more you craft your material to what seems to be their needs, the more hits and fewer misses you will score.

WHAT MAKES A GOOD STORY?

From a cynical point of view, a 'good story' is one which sells more newspapers. A story that sells papers is one that provides readers with information that is essential or important. There is nothing like news for selling newspapers is an old journalists' adage. It is true.

The problem with many press releases is that not only do they fail to contain a 'good' story, they contain no story at all. Of course, not every story can be a page one lead. Not every press release can make it into every publication you mail. But if you follow the five lessons below, you will achieve better results.

Lesson 1: make your story pass the 'so-what?' test
Don't push out a press release just because the managing director says he wants some publicity. Make sure you have a real story that will be of interest to the papers and magazines which will receive it. Too often this kind of release lands on an editor's desk:

Smith and Co is a well established engineering company that has been making widgets for 27 years. It has its factory at 27 Gasworks Road, Newcastle . . .

And so on. All background information, but not a news story in sight. This story fails what editors call the 'so-what? test'. Editors ask themselves these questions: what would happen if I left this story out? Would the readers be missing out on some vital information? If the answer to those questions is nothing and no respectively, your press release has failed the so-what? test. When you send a press release, you need to be sure the answer to both questions is yes.

Lesson 2: keep the story simple

The story needs to be obvious in the first sentence. Moreover, the editor needs to be able to see what the story is about in the first paragraph. As a press release writer, don't try to cram too much information into the first sentence. Decide what the story is and then make it clear.

For example, this is wrong:

Smith and Co, which has just opened its new factory in Newcastle, has appointed Mr Fred Smith as managing director to head the launch of the new range of widgets.

The problem with this as an opening sentence is that it contains three different stories:

- new factory
- new managing director
- new range of widgets.

Which story does the editor treat as most important? At the start, he realises there is a story here, but he is not sure which is the most important. Even more awkward, he might run separate columns or pages for new appointments, new products and companies moving site. He has to split the story up into segments to use it.

The correct way to deal with this is to write short separate releases for each of the stories. You can send all the stories together, but make sure that each stands on its own.

Lesson 3: make the story complete

A good story should answer questions, not leave them hanging in the air. When you write a story make sure that you provide all the information an editor needs to understand what is happening. You should:

- Give title, first name and surname of all people mentioned (the media doesn't like initials). For example: Mr Fred Smith, not F G Smith.

- Explain what position each person mentioned in the release holds in your organisation. The editor doesn't know that Fred Smith is the managing director.

- Provide full names of organisations, etc before reducing them to initials. A few specialists may know what the BDHF, BNF and ESRC are. Others need to be told they are the British Dental Health Foundation, British Nuclear Fuels and the Economic and Social Research Council. (Exceptions are those organisations that are known by their initials, such as the BBC.)

- Explain what each product is. Don't assume people know that the R2000 is a telephone handset.

Lesson 4: explain the context

It may be clear to you why your press release is an important story, but that doesn't mean it will be instantly clear to the journalist who receives it. The journalist may lack the background information needed to understand the context of the story.

If that is likely to be the case you need to provide enough information in your release to make the context clear without over-loading the story with background information. Indeed, in some cases the story may be completely hidden unless the context is clear.

For example:

Smith and Co has announced profits of £100,000 for the last financial year.

So what? A modest profit from a little known company, the editor will think. This version makes him sit up and take notice:

Smith and Co has announced profits of £100,000 for the last financial year, just 18 months after being rescued from the receiver by a new management team.

Suddenly, here is a bigger story — a turnaround story. The editor can see that far from £100,000 being a modest profit, it is a remarkable result for a company which a few months earlier had almost collapsed. By revealing the context, you make the story bigger.

You will need to help journalists understand the context of your stories in many cases when you are dealing with subjects that involve technical and specialised knowledge. If the journalist lacks the specialised knowledge, he is often unable to see the potential of the story. So tell him!

Lesson 5: make your story stand up

Editors often receive press releases that could make a story if only there were more facts to go on. For example:

> Smith and Co has won a £1m order from a major US banking organisation.

There could be a story here — a big order, a foreign customer, both strong story lines. But who is the customer? The fact is missing. Very often, when phoned by a journalist to fill in the information, the press officer will wail: 'The customer won't allow us to mention its name.'

That excuse won't wash with editors. Either you have a story or you don't. If you can't provide all the facts and figures you need to make your story stand up, forget it.

Action point

Have you ever issued a press release which didn't gain much coverage? If so, take another look at it in the light of the five lessons above. Could you have used any of the lessons to make the story stronger? Try redrafting it with those lessons in mind.

HOW TO MAKE A NEWS STORY

Your organisation may be awash with solid news stories but you may be short of stories to keep up a regular flow to your target publications. What can you do?

You can start to 'manufacture' some stories. As a general rule, action creates news, so you need to find ways to develop some news-making action. Here are some suggestions:

Run a survey

Newspapers and magazines love surveys because they reveal what people are thinking and doing. Besides, a well thought-out survey can reveal facts that weren't known before.

Find out what issues people in your market place feel strongly about.

Carry out the survey yourself or hire a market research organisation to do so. Link the results of your survey to actual problems faced by your customers. Publish the results of your survey in an attractive booklet format. Send out the results to the press and your customers.

Example
Compass, a food service management company, ran a survey called *The Lunchtime Report*. It was based on a survey of the lunching habits of workers in four European countries. The survey covered how much money workers spent on their lunch, what foods they most enjoyed, and how long they took for lunch. The survey provided good copy for a large number of newspapers and magazines.

Write a letter
You feel strongly about an issue — perhaps the tax rate on your product, new regulations planned by Brussels or the planning policies of the local council. Get your chairman or managing director to write a letter to the head of the relevant body. Release a copy of your letter to the press with a short covering release. (Don't do this until the recipient has received the letter. As a courtesy, mention in the letter that you will be releasing a copy to the press 'because the matter is of public interest'.)

Example
The heads of industry and trade bodies are constantly bombarding government departments with their view on topics of particular concern to them.

Sponsor a sport, theatre, concert, exhibition or book
The sponsorship will provide a financial boost for a worthy organisation and enable you to generate considerable new opportunities for press coverage on the back of your sponsorship.

You may think that sponsorship is only for the big battalions who sponsor national sporting events such as the Football League or Test Matches. It is possible to find worthwhile projects to sponsor at a more modest level.

But be aware that sponsorship is a two way deal. You should gain some business benefit for the cash you spend. This means you should choose a sponsorship project which is appropriate for your business.

Example
Many towns — such as Bath, Brighton and Edinburgh — have annual arts festivals. It is often possible to sponsor an individual event at the festival.

Although such sponsorship does not normally generate huge press coverage, it can create the kind of mentions in the press that your organisation might not have received.

Make a speech

Get your chairman, managing director or other leading executive to speak at an industry conference. Send an advance summary of the main points from the speech in a press release to the relevant publications.

Example

The Confederation of British Industry has an annual conference every October to which delegates from member companies go. It is possible for delegates from the floor to join in the debates, and sometimes they receive wide press coverage. If the CBI is too high-powered for you, start with your local Chamber of Commerce or industry federation.

Take part in an event

Form a football team for a local championship. Help with a charity. Take old age pensioners for a day by the sea. What you do will make news in local and, sometimes, trade publications. But a warning: you must be sincere about wanting to help in whatever it is you are involved with. Your assistance to a worthy cause comes first, the publicity spin-off second.

Example

Every year, London taxi drivers take handicapped children on a day out to the seaside. The event provides a great day out for kids and invariably picture stories in the national press for the normally maligned and abused cab drivers.

Play your part in a trade association or chamber of commerce

Your role will raise your profile and create more news opportunities.

Example

Consultants of one kind or another are often keen to play their part in industry and trade associations. Their membership provides them with a useful source of professional information, and also raises their profile.

THE ROLE OF THE GURU

One way to increase the number of opportunities for press coverage is by developing an industry 'guru' in your organisation. Most industries have their gurus — well known figures who are regularly invited by journalists to comment on developments in the industry. The guru is somebody who always has something to say, a comment to make, a useful fact to add to a journalist's story.

Journalists love gurus and couldn't manage well without them. When they need a quote or another point of view to strengthen a story, they know that the guru will be only too pleased to oblige.

If you can turn a senior executive in your company into a guru, you will open up many new opportunities for press coverage.

Gurus are usually people with long experience of their chosen industry. They will have served at senior levels, sometimes in several companies in the industry, sometimes for all of their career in just one. Often, they will also be a leading light in the industry trade association. They may speak regularly at trade conferences.

Perhaps there is somebody like that already in your company — and you had not recognised their guru potential. Perhaps you feel there is somebody who could be developed into a guru. If you are developing a guru from scratch, you must be prepared for a long haul. An individual does not become a guru overnight.

First, you must candidly ask: does the individual have guru potential? Test his or her guru qualities against the checklist below.

Checklist: Qualities needed by a good guru
- in a senior post
- presentable
- friendly
- knowledgeable about the broader issues in the industry
- good judgement
- clear thinking
- articulate
- not easily ruffled
- willing to be available to journalists.

Next, the would-be guru should embark on a programme of activity designed to raise his profile in his industry. He could do any of the following:

- Play a prominent role in his trade association.
- Speak at a conference.
- Write a pamphlet or book on industry or management issues.

- Go on an overseas study tour and report back.
- Write articles for the specialist press.
- Entertain journalists to lunch.
- Lobby politicians in his industry's interests.

One final point should not be left out of this list. He should ensure that he is playing his part in managing a successful company. A guru runs a successful company, not one teetering on the edge of bankruptcy.

Action point
Do you have a potential guru in your own organisation without realising it? Discuss potential candidates with colleagues. If someone is prepared to play the role of guru, make sure he or she is aware of the extra work burden this will impose.

Final thought: develop a nose for news
Ever heard the one about the rookie local reporter sent to cover the parish council meeting? Next morning, his news editor asked him where the copy was. 'Sorry,' he replied, 'the meeting didn't take place — the parish hall burned down.'

Here was one reporter who looked as though he had a bright future behind him — no nose for news. Stories crop up in the most unexpected places. And, sometimes, the most seemingly ordinary, even banal, events can make news. Study the papers, get to know what they want and you'll develop a nose for news.

It is one of the most valuable attributes a press officer possesses. But remember this caveat — the news you release must serve your organisation's interests.

5
Building a Story
Step by Step

'Literature is the art of writing something that will be read twice; journalism what will be grasped at once.' — Cyril Connolly, *Enemies of Promise.*

And, Connolly might have added in the case of press releases, grasped within 10 seconds.

We live in a world of instant and fleeting images. You might not think of that press release over which you have expended so much creative sweat as a 'fleeting image'. But to an editor it is just part of a pile of bumph on his desk that has to be shifted before he can move on to the other work of the day.

Editors know that most of the press releases in their morning pile will be rubbish — either non-stories or poorly targeted material that could be of interest to some other journal but not to them. So if you can provide some real news, it appears from the pile like a rare orchid on a rubbish tip.

ESSENTIAL ELEMENTS OF A PRESS RELEASE

A press release is essentially a news story written to interest a specific publication or group of publications. It consists of three main parts:

- The headline
- The introduction (often called by journalists the 'intro')
- The body of the story.

Sometimes a press release may also contain a 'note to editors' which is added at the end. The purpose of the note to editors is to provide background information about the company or product mentioned. Information in the note is not material that should be in the story, but extra information that a journalist who is not familiar with your organisation might need to know.

Although the headline comes at the top of the story, you should write it last. In this way, you ensure that the headline reflects the story rather than twisting the story to justify the headline. So we shall discuss head-lines after talking about the introduction and the body of the story.

CHOOSING THE RIGHT INFORMATION

However, even before you start to write the press release, you need to collect together your information and select the main facts you need. You also need to pitch your story at the right level for the publications you are aiming it at. These two tasks are interlinked.

After completing the interview(s) (see page 36) you should have a mass of facts which you could use in the press release. Which ones should you select and how should you use them?

If you follow these rules, you won't go far wrong.

First step: make the facts answer the W questions

These are the what, who, where, why and when. If the facts you choose don't answer those questions, you will probably leave loose ends in your story. The story must tell:

what	is happening
who	is doing it
where	it is taking place
when	it happened or will happen
why	it is happening.

Let us consider a couple of examples.

Example One

Gobble and Belch, a food processing company, has decided to launch a new range of baby food for discriminating infants in a test market in London and the south east. It will be called Gourmet Infant. The company's research revealed that the modern baby likes a range of subtle flavours. Gobble and Belch plans to have its first three products in the range out for Christmas. That information can be analysed using the five Ws this way:

what	Gourmet Infant baby food range launched.
who	By Gobble and Belch.
where	In London and the south east.
when	In time for Christmas.
why	Research reveals modern babies have sophisticated palates.

Example Two

Megamoney Bank, with 3,000 nationwide branches, has launched its own Gold Card, available to people with incomes of more than £30,000 a year. The bank says the card will attract more professional and business customers.

what	Gold Card launched.
who	By Megamoney Bank.
where	Whole of UK.
when	Now.
why	To win more professional and business customers.

Action point

Now analyse the information in the same format as the above two examples for the following story: Flyaway Holidays is to offer a special holiday for water sports enthusiasts on the Black Sea. The tour company will use a new water sports complex built by the Bulgarian Government. The first holidaymakers will fly out next summer and the holiday will be available in the next brochure, published in November. (See the answer at the end of this chapter.)

In these examples, the facts you have chosen form the core of the story. Without these facts, it is impossible to understand what is happening. So these facts will form the introduction of the story. They will appear in the first paragraph.

However, most readers will want more detail than the bare facts. So you need to select more detail to add into your story.

Second step: choose facts to build up the story

The second step is to choose facts to build up the story so that you pitch your press release at the right level for the publication you aim it at. Take the Gobble and Belch story, for example. That could be written as a release for

● national newspapers (especially women's pages) and those women's magazines aimed at married women

● the trade press covering grocery and supermarket outlets

● regional newspapers in London and the south east.

Each will need a different treatment founded on a different selection and use of facts. If you were writing that story, you might find, apart from those already given, the following facts among your notes:

(a) 1.5m babies eat canned baby food in UK

(b) 23% in London and the south east

(c) market research estimates gourmet foods could capture 14% of sales

(d) asparagus, lobster and paté de fois gras were three most popular choices in market surveys

(e) 800 supermarkets will stock range in trials

(f) parents buy 14 cans of baby food per baby a week

(g) launch of Gourmet Infant will be backed with £750,000 advertising campaign on television and regional press

(h) a professor of nutrition hired by the food company said eating gourmet foods would encourage children to eat a more balanced diet in later life

(i) 50% of mothers in a market survey said a baby should have at least one special treat meal a week

(j) special point of sale containers and advertising material will be provided to stockists

(k) the market research for the product was conducted in Bromley, Basingstoke and Chichester.

Some of those facts you would use in all three releases, for the national, trade and regional papers, but others would be used in only one or two of the releases.

Action point
Go through the list and mark which facts you would select for the

    women's magazine release   _____
    south east newspapers release   _____
    retailer's trade press release.   _____

Then check your selection against that suggested at the end of this chapter.

QUESTION AND ANSWER

Question: What can I do when many people want to get involved with writing the release and they all have their own ideas about what should be in it?

Answer: As we have seen in Chapter 2, you should have set up a proper approval structure for press releases so that everybody knows what their rights and responsibilities are. If people insist on becoming more involved, invite them to submit their own suggested draft to you. Often, this will put them off. If it doesn't, you can use material from their draft, if relevant, in the release you write.

ORGANISING THE INFORMATION FOR EASY WRITING

Having disentangled the facts you want to put in your release, how should you organise the information so that you can use it easily and naturally as you write your release? The golden rule of all press releases is: *Always get the story into the first sentence.* This ought to be obvious, but many press releases do not achieve it.

The most common faults are:

● Putting in background information about the company which should be left for much later in the story.

> *Example:* Gobble and Belch, the Nowheretown food manufacturer that was founded 83 years ago by the grandfather of the managing director, is launching a new range of baby food.

Everything between the commas in that opening sentence is background information and should be left for later in the story.

● Describing the thinking leading up to the launch of the new product (or whatever the real story is).

> *Example:* Gobble and Belch, the food manufacturer, has been researching the market in baby foods. The company felt that there should be a wider choice of foods for mothers to buy for their babies. Research showed that a large percentage of mothers agreed. As a result, the company's product developers set to work . . .

And so on, and so on. Eventually, after half a dozen or more paragraphs we get to the point — that Gobble and Belch is launching a new range of baby food.

● Telling an anecdote which is secondary to the main story.

> *Example:* One day John Taylor, managing director of Gobble and Belch, received an interesting letter from a Manchester mother. She said that her baby had developed an unusual taste for paté de fois gras. This started Mr Taylor thinking.

Again, the main point is buried further down the story. Just possibly an anecdote could get an editor reading, but it better be a stronger story than this and it better get to the point quickly. If there is an interesting anecdote, use it further down the story.

● Attempts at light-hearted banter, presumably with the intention of putting the editor reading the story in a good mood.

> *Example:* Cheer up you chubby-faced infants. Here's a tea-time treat.

Ugh! If the journalist wants to write this stuff, let him do it himself. Your task is to supply the facts to help him.

In terms of organising your information, this means understanding what your story is. The what, who, where, why and when exercise should help here. One way to do this is to write down the five Ws in the manner described earlier. Then you should make sure that they are all covered in the first two sentences.

Selecting other information

What about the supporting information? When you have disentangled the facts you need from the mass of information you have collected, it helps to jot them down as a simple list on a sheet of scrap paper. Initially, don't bother too much about the order in which you write them.

Look at the list you have created. Ask yourself the question: have I got

ntually, after **half** a dozen or more paragraphs
Gobble and **Belch** is launching a new range of

'hich is secondary to the main story.

---

hn Taylor, managing director of Gobble
an interesting letter from a Manchester
her baby had developed an unusual taste
This started Mr Taylor thinking.

---

uried further down the story. Just possibly an
or reading, but it better be a stronger story than
e point quickly. If there is an interesting anec-
the story.

rted banter, presumably with the intention of
ding the story in a good mood.

---

ou chubby-faced infants. Here's a tea-time

---

ts to write this stuff, let him do it himself. Your
to help him.

g your information, this means understanding
hat, who, where, why and when exercise should
this is to write down the five Ws in the manner
ou should make sure that they are all covered in

nation

g information? When you have disentangled the
mass of information you have collected, it helps
ple list on a sheet of scrap paper. Initially, don't
e order in which you write them.
ve created. Ask yourself the question: have I got

Example Two
Megamoney Bank, with 3,000 nationwide branches, has launched its own
Gold Card, available to people with incomes of more than £30,000 a year.
The bank says the card will attract more professional and business customers.

what	Gold Card launched.
who	By Megamoney Bank.
where	Whole of UK.
when	Now.
why	To win more professional and business customers.

Action point

Now analyse the information in the same format as the above two
examples for the following story: Flyaway Holidays is to offer a special
holiday for water sports enthusiasts on the Black Sea. The tour company
will use a new water sports complex built by the Bulgarian Government.
The first holidaymakers will fly out next summer and the holiday will be
available in the next brochure, published in November. (See the answer
at the end of this chapter.)

In these examples, the facts you have chosen form the core of the story.
Without these facts, it is impossible to understand what is happening. So
these facts will form the introduction of the story. They will appear in the
first paragraph.

However, most readers will want more detail than the bare facts. So
you need to select more detail to add into your story.

Second step: choose facts to build up the story

The second step is to choose facts to build up the story so that you pitch your
press release at the right level for the publication you aim it at. Take the
Gobble and Belch story, for example. That could be written as a release for

● national newspapers (especially women's pages) and those
  women's magazines aimed at married women

● the trade press covering grocery and supermarket outlets

● regional newspapers in London and the south east.

Each will need a different treatment founded on a different selection
and use of facts. If you were writing that story, you might find, apart from
those already given, the following facts among your notes:

(a) 1.5m babies eat canned baby food in UK

(b) 23% in London and the south east

(c) market research estimates gourmet foods could capture 14% of sales

(d) asparagus, lobster and paté de fois gras were three most popular choices in market surveys

(e) 800 supermarkets will stock range in trials

(f) parents buy 14 cans of baby food per baby a week

(g) launch of Gourmet Infant will be backed with £750,000 advertising campaign on television and regional press

(h) a professor of nutrition hired by the food company said eating gourmet foods would encourage children to eat a more balanced diet in later life

(i) 50% of mothers in a market survey said a baby should have at least one special treat meal a week

(j) special point of sale containers and advertising material will be provided to stockists

(k) the market research for the product was conducted in Bromley, Basingstoke and Chichester.

Some of those facts you would use in all three releases, for the national, trade and regional papers, but others would be used in only one or two of the releases.

Action point
Go through the list and mark which facts you would select for the

women's magazine release   _____
south east newspapers release   _____
retailer's trade press release.   _____

Then check your selection against that suggested at the end of this chapter.

QUESTION

Question: Wh
writing the rel
be in it?
   Answer: As
approval struc
rights and re
involved, invi
this will put th
if relevant, in

ORGANISIN

Having disent
you organise
you write you
get the story
press releases
   The most

● Putting
    should b

Example
facturer
managin

Everything b
information

● Describ
    (or wha

Exampl
research
there sh
their ba
agreed.
work .

And so on, and so
we get to the point
baby food.

● Telling an ane

Example: One
and Belch, rec
mother. She sa
for paté de fois

Again, the main po
anecdote could get a
this and it better get
dote, use it further d

● Attempts at lig
    putting the edit

Example: Cheer
treat.

Ugh! If the journalist
task is to supply the
   In terms of organ
what your story is. Th
help here. One way to
described earlier. The
the first two sentences

Selecting other inf
What about the suppo
facts you need from th
to jot them down as a
bother too much about
   Look at the list you

all the information I need to write this story? If not, go back to your notes and other background information and search for more supporting facts.

You need to bear in mind the weight of the release you plan to write. How strong a story is it? Will it need two paragraphs or two pages? Plainly, you will need considerably more information for the latter. In general, a press release should be less than two pages, unless it is a story of considerable weight or a technical story sent to a specialist publication which will require a lot of detail.

In the shortest of stories, you probably won't need much more than the what, who, where, when and why information.

Example: Gobble and Belch today opened its new south-east regional office at 15 High Street, Croydon, Surrey. The office is coordinating the regional launch of the Gourmet Infant baby food products.

Two sentences say it all, and not many publications will be interested in much more detail. Press release writers often think a short press release looks thin. They are tempted to build it up with extra words, usually background information of no news value. This is a mistake. Journalists are quite capable of judging the weight of a story and are happier to have a story worth two paragraphs told in two paragraphs than in a page and a half.

In longer stories, you will need to organise more information. In this case, you should arrange the information you have collected in order of importance. In almost all cases, you should use the information in your press release in descending order of importance.

But of importance to whom? To the person reading the press release is the short answer. What you must try to do is to look at the facts you have in your list through the eyes of the editors to whom you will send the release. Bear in mind that the editor will want answers to questions such as:

● what is new?
● what is unusual?
● what does the reader need to know in order to understand what is happening?
● which people or organisations will be affected by this?
● how will they be affected?

Judge the facts you have on your list against those sorts of criteria and mark them up in a rough order of importance. At the same time, group those facts you will want to use in the same paragraphs together.

When you have done this, you are ready to start writing the release.

QUESTION AND ANSWER

Question: What should I do when I find that I lack significant facts to write the release?

Answer: Go back to your sources to get the information you need. Don't try to write a story with holes in it. If your sources are not prepared to divulge significant facts, you have to ask yourself whether you really have a story.

WRITING FIRST PARAGRAPHS WITH POWER

The biggest single fault with press releases is that the first paragraph kills the story — if there is a story. It cannot be said often enough: always, always, always get the story in the first paragraph.

But what is 'the story'? Quite simply, the story is the most interesting or most important or most unusual thing you have to say from the point of view of the publication receiving the release. This means that the same facts can be used to tell a fresh story for different publications. What might make an interesting piece for one paper would go straight into the bin in another.

In deciding what is the story, it helps to think of the five Ws. One of those Ws is more important than the rest. It forms the main point of your story. If what is happening is most important, make that the main point of the story. If who is doing it is more important, put that first.

In other words, you can think of each press release you write as a:

* *what* story
* *who* story
* *when* story
* *where* story
* *why* story

Let us examine that point with the help of our old friends Gobble and Belch. The gourmet baby food story would need to be written up in different ways for the women's, trade and local press, using different information. Most significant, the opening paragraphs could be quite different.

Action point

Look at these three possible opening sentences for a trade paper, a local paper and a women's magazine. Which is for which?

(a) Mothers chose the recipes for Gourmet Infant, a new range of tinned baby foods launched this week by Gobble and Belch. (A *what* story.)

(b) Gobble and Belch this week launched a test market of Gourmet Infant, its new range of tinned baby foods, in 800 supermarkets in London and the south-east. (A *who* story.)

(c) Chichester was chosen by market researchers to test Gourmet Infant, a new range of tinned baby foods, launched by Gobble and Belch. (A *where* story.)

Check your answers at the end of the chapter.

It is worth adding that a *when* story would start like this:

'A pre-Christmas launch for Gobble and Belch's Gourmet Infant range of baby food will give youngsters the chance to sample the recipes over the holiday period.'

And a why story could read like this:

'In a move to promote healthy eating patterns among babies, Gobble and Belch is launching a range of gourmet baby food.'

These last two examples feel slightly strained because the story is not a natural when or why story. If the introduction to your release feels strained, perhaps you have misjudged the type of story you are writing. Look at it again.

The secret of the opening sentence is to select the facts from those you have available that will be of most interest to the editor. The women's magazine, for example, will not be interested in details of the test marketing. But a women's magazine editor would probably be interested in the fact that a food company asked mothers to choose the recipes for a new range of baby food. Similarly, the local paper story extracts the one local angle from the story and builds everything else around it.

One way to test whether you have written a strong opening sentence for your release is to ask whether the first few words of the sentence would make an editor read more. Look at the three sentences in the action point example:

(a) 'Mothers chose the recipes. . .'
(b) 'Gobble and Belch this week launched a test market. . .'
(c) 'Chichester was chosen by market researchers. . .'

In each case, the release hits the editor right between the eyes with a relevant and targeted piece of information.

BUILDING UP THE STORY STEP BY STEP

No press release ever 'writes itself'. But if you draft the first paragraph well, you will find it much easier to write the rest of the story. Apart from any other consideration, you will have a clear idea in your own mind what the story is.

We have already seen how you select the relevant facts to put into the story. You should use them in the order of most importance — the significant facts at the start of the story, the less important further down.

Always remember the five Ws — what, who, where, when and why. You should have answered those questions in the first two or three sentences. But the five Ws are relevant to the whole of the release. You need to provide more detail on them as you develop your story:

● *What:* provide all the information you need for the editor to under-stand what is happening. Add extra relevant facts.

● *Who:* provide more detail about the who, whether an organisation or person.

● *Where:* build in extra relevant facts about the location, if they help the story along.

● *When:* make sure you have been sufficiently precise in your opening paragraph. If more explanation is needed, provide it later in the story.

● *Why:* this often provides the explanation of what is happening, and the reasons behind it.

When writing your story, bear in mind that although the five Ws should be in almost all stories, they will not carry the same weight in each story. Indeed, if you write the story in different ways, the balance of importance between the Ws can change from one version of the story to another.

HEADLINE NEWS

As we have already seen, the headline is the last part of the release you should write — not the first. Until you have drafted the release, you will not have a clear idea of the story.

The headline should sum up the essence of the story. Often it will draw on key words from the first sentence of the story. It should immediately show an editor what the story is about. The headline is certainly the first part of the release he will read. Sometimes it is the only part of the release he will read.

It is forgiveable to stop an editor reading with a headline which reveals the story as one of no interest. It is unforgiveable to lose the editor with a headline which hides the contents of a story which would have been of interest had he read past it.

Good rules for headline-writing
In order to write good headlines, follow these rules:

Keep it short
A headline is a summary and attention grabber. Ten words is maximum. Incredibly, some releases carry multiple headlines running to more than 100 words. That is not a headline but an essay.

Keep it simple
That means expressing the main point of the release as a simple idea. What is the central point of the release? Find it and then put it in the headline.

Use short words
Headline writers have to make their headlines fit the space available. Normally they like short words. Short words also convey ideas more simply (see above). If necessary, use a thesaurus to find the short words you need.

Put a verb in it
A verb is an action word. It brings a headline to life and gives the (hopefully) correct impression that something new is happening. So don't write: 'Gobble and Belch's new office'. Write: 'Gobble and Belch opens new office'.

Don't try to be funny or clever
There is nothing worse than a half-baked pun topping a weak story. In any event, the headline you write is unlikely to be used. Sub-editors will write their own headlines. If they think a 'funny' headline is appropriate they will write their own.

Action point
Bearing in mind the above rules, rewrite these headlines. Then compare your version with those at the end of this chapter.

(a) Gobble and Belch has launched a new range of baby food called Gourmet Infant.
(b) Smith criticises local authority development proposals.
(c) Babies to gobble company's new food.
(d) Company's new food range.

HOW TO GIVE A STORY 'TOP SPIN'

'Top spin' is a phrase that has crept into journalists' vocabulary over the last few years. Nobody has ever defined it with perfect precision, but it broadly means giving a story an extra twist to make it more interesting.

Of course, some of the fish-and-chip tabloids interpret that to mean as many twists as necessary to make the story 'stand up'. With the result that the story bears about as much relation to fact as Noddy and Big Ears. But we shouldn't allow the sleazy side of newspapers to put us off using a journalistic technique which is perfectly reputable when used honourably.

There is nothing wrong with making a story more interesting by the way you tell it. So just what is top spin? And how can you use it in press releases?

First, let us clearly establish what it is not. It is not puffery, self praise or exaggeration. Yet these find their way into a high proportion of press releases. Typical examples of each are:

● Puffery: 'Gobble and Belch, whose baby foods have been eaten by infants for three generations, has established itself as a leading supplier of nourishing and tasty meals for the nation's youngsters. . .' Etcetera, etcetera. Puffery is words that lengthen a story but get it nowhere.

● Self praise: 'Gobble and Belch produces the best baby foods from the finest ingredients. . .' Who says so? Gobble and Belch, apparently. In the words of Mandy Rice-Davis, they would, wouldn't they. Who cares? Certainly not the editors who will receive these platitudes.

● Exaggeration: 'Millions of mothers thank God for Gobble and Belch every day, as they open a tin of. . .' Ugh! Are the nation's mums really down on their knees in the kitchen as they prepare their toddler's tea? No editor will fall for that.

Top spin is a way of looking for the 'pressure points' in a story that will make it more interesting to the reader — and the editor who receives your press release. Often, giving a story some top spin involves finding a suitable 'peg' to hang the story on. In other words, a reason for the story.

Here are four ways to add top spin to a story:

Timing

A story that might make an editor yawn one week could make him sit up and take notice another. Just as there is a season for salmon fishing and grouse shooting, so there is for certain kinds of stories. For example, newspapers will be carrying Christmas shopping stories in the couple of weeks before Christmas.

Example

Peterborough Software, a company which sells computer systems that help companies administer their payrolls, sent out a press release about the problems and costs caused to companies by staff taking unofficial days off over the Christmas period. The release was sent out a few days before Christmas. Normally, a story about absenteeism would rate little or no news value to the national press, but the *Financial Times* picked it up and ran it on its front page.

Event

There are plenty of events during the year that can provide a peg for a story. They include sporting events such as the Cup Final, Wimbledon and the Derby and regular dates in the nation's calendar, such as the opening of Parliament or Budget Day. At these times, editors will be looking for stories which they can use in their coverage of these events.

Example

On Budget Day, leading firms of accountants vie with each other to rush out their comments on the contents of the budget.

Issue

Plenty of issues come and go. Inflation, environmentalism, the plight of the inner cities — these and many others are the constant concern of journalists. By linking your story to such an issue you drive home its relevance, link it to what is happening in the wider world and make it seem less parochial.

Example

Stung by public complaints about the poor quality of water, many of the privatised water companies spend a significant amount of their press relations effort in finding and releasing stories about their activities in cleaning up the water system and reducing pollution.

Conflict

Conflict makes news. You may think that becoming involved in conflict raises the risk of bad publicity for your organisation. Perhaps, in some cases, it does. But by letting your views be known, you also convey to your public the kind of values your organisation believes in.

Example

In the summer of 1992, Sir Christopher Tugendhat, chairman of the Abbey National bank (and a former *Financial Times* journalist), put forward a plan to kick-start the then sluggish housing market. He suggested the Government should pay tax credits to people who had to sell their houses at a loss because of falling property values. Sir Christopher's plan brought him front-page coverage in most national newspapers. Although many newspapers criticised the details of the plan, there was widespread praise for his initiative in stimulating discussion on the issue. Abbey National presented itself as a company caring about the predicament of millions of home owners.

DEALING WITH SPECIAL CASES

In 19 cases out of 20 — possibly more — it is enough to send a single story in a single press release. But there are some special cases. For example, what happens when the amount of information you have to provide is just too large for one release? What happens when journalists need a large amount of background information about your organisation?

The backgrounder

The backgrounder is a special kind of press release which is designed to provide (as the name suggests) simple background facts about the organisation. It tends to be used in two ways:

● to reply to journalists who request background information about the company;

● to send with a press release when the journalists receiving it will definitely need to know more about your organisation in order to understand the context of the story.

Although the backgrounder does not contain a specific news story, it still needs to be presented in a professional way and provide all the background information a journalist might need.

There are two main types of backgrounder:

- company or organisation backgrounder
- technical backgrounder

The company backgrounder provides information about the company or organisation. The technical information fills out the technical detail of a product which may be mentioned in an accompanying news release — for example a computer, a car, a piece of machinery.

Each backgrounder needs to contain different kinds of information. See the two checklists below.

Checklist: information needed in a corporate backgrounder
- name of company/organisation
- address and telephone number
- whether public or private
- when founded
- size: *ie* turnover, employees, branches, members
- main products and services/activities
- main markets
- leading managers/officers
- main business partners, if any
- sample customers/users

Checklist: information needed in a technical backgrounder
- name of product
- when launched
- main elements of technical specification
- what is new in latest version of the product
- distribution/retailing of product
- target end-users
- price
- sample users

The press pack

What is a **press pack** and when should you send one? A press pack is a collection of information sent to journalists. It generally includes a mixture of multiple press releases, fact sheets, brochures, press cuttings, photographs and annual reports. Press packs have been known to weigh several pounds. Yet the news value of a press pack is usually in inverse proportion to its weight.

You should only send a press pack when the news value of the announcement truly warrants it. This could be when:

● You launch several products at the same time and each needs its own press release.

● You announce a batch of new appointments at the same time with separate press releases and photographs.

● You announce your annual results, when you need to send the annual report as well as a news release and financial results summary.

● You launch a major product which requires a main release, technical backgrounder, photographs and, possibly, other information.

● You are involved in a joint venture, merger or acquisition with another company when each needs to send its press release and corporate backgrounder.

Obey this golden rule of press packs: only put in other documents such as brochures, press cuttings and so on if they are essential to the journalist understanding the story. A journalist does not have time to read a huge pile of background material and you could put him off by hiding your story among a mass of marginal background bumph.

Problem and remedy

Problem: The sales manager says we have to include a sales brochure every time we send out a press release on a product. Should I agree?

Remedy: There is no harm in sending a sales brochure when you launch a new product, but you don't need to send one every time you issue a story about the product. Explain to the sales manager that journalists need a story not a sales message.

Action points: suggested answers

Flyaway Holidays

What:	Holiday for water sports enthusiasts
Who:	Flyaway Holidays
Where:	Black Sea
When:	Available in November
Why:	Because Bulgarian government has opened a new water sports centre.

Gobble and Belch three releases
Facts for women's magazine release: a, d, f, h, i.
Facts for south-east newspapers release: a, b, d, h, k.
Facts for retailers' trade press release: a, c, d, e, f, g, i, j, k.

Three opening sentences
a = women's magazine; b = trade paper; c = local paper

Wrong headlines
(a) Gobble and Belch launches Gourmet Infant
     (Original: too many words.)

(b) Smith attacks council plan
     (Original: too many long words.)

(c) New food launched for babies
     (Original: dreadful pun.)

(d) Company launches gourmet food range
     (Original: no verb.)

Final thought: can't put it down

What is it that gives a book a 'can't put it down' feeling? Usually, it is the fact that you are so intrigued or fascinated by what has already happened that you want to know more. There can be an element of that in the best press releases. How does it work? Put a 'hook' into every paragraph — a piece of information which has to be amplified later on. That keeps people reading. But be careful you don't make your release read like a thriller. You must not deliberately withhold key facts, rather present the needed information in such a way that the reader wants to know more. If you can do this, it is a great skill.

6
Putting on the (Right) Style

'Journalism is the only job that requires no degrees, no diplomas and no specialised knowledge of any kind.' — Patrick Campbell, *My Life and Easy Times*.

Of course, nowadays you *can* get a university degree in journalism, but there is no evidence that those who do make better journalists than those who come up the harder way. Certainly, you don't need any degree or diploma to perform an effective job as a press release writer.

But you do need some specialised knowledge. Some of that knowledge is concerned with the style in which press releases should be presented, written and distributed. This chapter deals with all three.

FIRST IMPRESSIONS

We have already seen that first impressions are important to an editor. If your press release turns up on scruffy paper, with three typos and a grammatical error in the first sentence, he will be far less likely to read on.

You need to think about the presentation of your press release under a number of headings:

The paper
This should be A4 sized — the same size as standard notepaper. It is not essential for the front sheet to be printed, but it does no harm. If you plan to print press release paper, keep the design simple and the amount of information printed on the paper to a minimum. You don't want the press release paper cluttered up with names of directors, branch offices, company brand names, Queen's Award to Industry logos and other irrelevant matter.

The ideal press release paper contains the company name and logo, head office address, telephone and fax numbers and prominently the words 'News Release' or 'Press Release' according to your taste — and that is about it. All that information should be confined to the top quarter of the paper. Some press release papers go in for fancy designs which either snake round the page or are printed as a background tint over the whole page. Forget it. Graphic designers may like that kind of thing. Journalists don't. Figure 7 shows four good examples of press release paper headings.

There is no need to have any printed matter on follow-on sheets used in press releases. Some companies use elaborately printed follow-on sheets. They might as well have saved their money.

Indeed, there is no need to have printed press release paper at all. It is quite enough to have the words 'News Release' or 'Press Release' typed prominently at the top of the page along with the name of your organisation. You can even combine the two in a heading such as: News from the Anytown Women's Institute.

Whether you use printed stationery or not, make sure the paper is of reasonable quality. If your story is used, the release may come in for some rough handling from sub-editors. Journalists will become increasingly irritated by paper which tears or is easily punctured by biros as it is sub-edited.

Ideally, the paper should be white, although light coloured tints would be just about acceptable. But do not use dark coloured papers as it is harder to read the text. Equally, the paper should have a matt finish. Press releases should not be printed on gloss paper, as this is difficult to write on.

If there is more than one page to your release, the pages should be neatly stapled together. There was a time when the rule was never to staple the pages of a release but paper-clip them together. In fact, paper-clips have largely fallen out of use because they are not very practical in news offices where piles of stories are handled. The paper-clips come off or pages from other stories mysteriously work their way under the clip holding another.

WORDS ON A PAGE

The next question to address is layout. How should the words appear on the page? The most important point is that your press release should be laid out so that sub-editors can easily process it into the newspaper. They need to edit the copy and make type marks on it for the typesetter. They won't be able to do that if the words are crammed together so that there is hardly an inch of white space anywhere.

Your release should be typed double spaced on one side of the paper. There should be a margin at least an inch wide on either side. Ideally, the headline should be placed about one-third of the way down

Health & Safety Commission

CABINET OFFICE
Office of Public Service and Science

NEWS RELEASE

P·E International
The Management and Computer Consultants

NEWS RELEASE

CMG — Computer Management Group

PRESS RELEASE
PERSBERICHT
PRESS MITTEILUNG
COMMUNIQUÉ DE PRESSE

Fig. 7. Some good examples of press release headings. From the top: HSC's classic design with a hint of urgency, Cabinet Office's stately officialdom, P-E International's workmanlike consultancy, CMG's international touch.

the first page and the copy should start about half way down the first page. This leaves plenty of room for the sub-editor to write in his own headline and other instructions to the typesetter. (Figure 8 shows an ideal layout for the first page of a press release.) If using a word processor, the best pitch is about 10 characters to the inch, although 12 is acceptable. But avoid the denser pitches such as 15, which usually involve using smaller type faces.

The first paragraph of your story should not be indented. Subsequent paragraphs should be indented. There is no need to leave a line between paragraphs as you might do if typing a letter. You should not carry over a paragraph from one page to another.

Each page of your release should have a **catchline**. This is one word that identifies the subject of the story. For example, in a new appointment release the name of the person concerned. The catchline should contain the key word followed by three leaders (dots) and the page number. At the bottom of each page write 'mf' for more follows. At the finish of the story write the word 'ends' to show there is no more.

After the word 'ends', you need to give details of where and from whom a journalist can get more information. So add the words 'For further information' and then supply a name and telephone number. In some cases, you may want to supply more than one name and telephone number.

Is all this important? Yes, for by laying out your press release you are making the information in it more accessible. And anything that makes the information easier to use will increase the chances of your release making column inches.

Problem and remedy

Problem: Our typists seem to produce press releases that look like any other company report. What can I do about it?

Remedy: Speak to the office manager to explain the special needs of press releases. Win the manager's cooperation in developing your own press release style. Explain why you need releases typed in a way that is acceptable to journalists. When the manager understands the need, he or she will be more ready to help.

WRITING IN GOOD NEWS STYLE

You want to write your press release so that it sounds like a story especially written for the publication to which you are sending it. In this way, the editor or sub-editor will immediately feel at home with the release as soon as he starts to read it. If you are to do this, you will need

HOW TO BOOKS LTD

PRESS RELEASE

Issued: 3 January 199X

Guide. . . 1

NEW GUIDE FOR PRESS RELEASE WRITERS PUBLISHED

A guide for people who write press releases was published today by How To Books. The paperback, Writing a Press Release, is authored by Peter Bartram, a writer and journalist.

The book covers all the stages of planning and executing a press relations campaign. Chapters cover how to find stories for press releases, how to target releases to relevant publications, and how to write stories step by step.

There are also chapters on good press release writing style and distributing releases. The reader also finds tips on using photographs and graphics to support press releases.

m.f. . .

Fig. 8. Correct layout for the first page of a press release.

to study the styles of the different publications to which you will be sending material. In general there will be few major differences. If you follow some well established rules, you will not go far wrong.

Keep sentences short

Quite simply, information given in short sentences is easier to understand than the same information given in long sentences. But that doesn't mean that all sentences have to be the same monotonous length. As a general rule, no sentence should run to more than about 25 words, perhaps 30 in exceptional circumstances. A good average is around 15 words per sentence. (The sentences in this paragraph have 19, 14, 19, 9 and 13 words.)

See from the example below how short sentences help you get a simple story across more easily. A long sentence version might run:

'John Smith, who was deputy chief executive of Tasty Grub, has been appointed managing director of Gobble and Belch, the baby food manufacturer whose head office is in Anytown, and he will be taking up his new position on Monday 1 July.'

In all, 42 in one sentence. How much crisper is:

'John Smith becomes the new managing director of Gobble and Belch on Monday 1 July. He joins the Anytown baby food manufacturer from Tasty Grub, where he was deputy chief executive.'

Two sentences, with 15 words and 16 words respectively, overall nine words less than the first version, with nothing of significance lost. Moreover, the important point, that Smith is joining Gobble and Belch, rather than that he is leaving Tasty Grub, is in the first sentence.

Action point

Now try turning this long opener into a crisper intro with two sentences:

'How To Books, based in Oxford, has published 'Writing a Press Release' this week, which has been written by Peter Bartram, a writer and journalist who is the author of more than 2,500 articles for magazines and 19 books.'

Compare your version with the one at the end of this chapter.

Keep paragraphs short

Press release writers should remember the advice given in *Fowler's Modern English Usage*: 'The purpose of the paragraph is to give the reader a rest. The writer is saying to him: "Have you got that? If so, I'll go on to the next point."'

In press releases, paragraphs should be kept short. In general, not more than two or three sentences per paragraph. Four or five is certainly the maximum, but try to avoid single sentence paragraphs. Often the one sentence paragraph could have been attached to the paragraph before or the one after.

As Fowler says: 'Paragraphing is also a matter of the eye. A reader will address himself more readily to his task if he sees from the start that he will have breathing-spaces from time to time than if what is before him looks like a marathon course.' Too true.

Stick to the facts

The editor wants to find the facts as quickly as possible. That is made more difficult if the facts are hidden away behind puffery and self-congratulation. In writing terms, this means beware of using too many (even any) adjectives and adverbs. Does the adjective you are about to use really add to the facts of the story?

Unfortunately, most press releases descend into some degree of puffery. It seems that press release writers simply cannot resist it. Or perhaps they are talked into it by other managers. After all, you naturally believe that your product is the best in the market, so why not say so? Unfortunately, you are taking a subjective rather than an objective view.

It is admittedly difficult to be objective when you are so close to your company and its products. But it helps when writing press releases if you are aware of the danger words which show you may be drifting away from the facts. The checklist below warns you of some of the danger words in press releases. If you find yourself using one, you need to ask yourself whether somebody else would use the word, knowing nothing about your company, product or service. If the answer is no, cut it out.

Checklist: 12 puff words and phrases to avoid in press releases
   Unique
   Leading
   Fastest
   Flexible
   Easy to use
   Popular
   World class
   Successful
   Breakthrough
   Major
   Versatile
   Key

Here is an actual example of what happens when you don't stick to the facts. This is taken from a real press release but the names are changed to protect the guilty.

'Following the *unquestionable success and growth* of ABC Ltd during the past year, brought about *in no small way* by their attendance at CIM 91, the company's *vast knowledge and expertise* will once again be accessible to the British manufacturing industry at the CIM '92.'

The story here (if there is one) seems to be that ABC will be exhibiting at CIM '92. So why not say so? The story is also killed by the self-congratulatory puffery (the words in italics) which would seem over-blown in an advertisement or brochure.

Another problem: nowhere in the release does the writer say what CIM '92 is (presumably an exhibition) or when and where it takes place. Perhaps many of the recipients of this release will know what CIM '92 is and when and where it happens, but this writer, at least, didn't.

Question and answer

Question: How can I handle the situation when another manager insists on including self-congratulatory puffery in a press release?

Answer: Ask him whether he wants to see his story in print. If he does, he will want to produce a press release that is acceptable to a journalist.

Gauge the story weight

How long should your press release be? That depends largely on the weight or strength of the story. This is not an easy question to answer, because the same story will have a different weight in different publications. For example, a new appointment press release might make three lines in the *Financial Times*, three sentences in the local paper where the new appointee lives, and three paragraphs in a trade publication.

One way to tackle this problem is to ensure that the story is in the first sentence and that the press release can be cut from the end. In this way, any publication can take as much copy as it chooses, starting from the first paragraph.

But you still need to make a judgement about how much copy to provide. The sensible approach is to look at the publications to which you will be sending the release and make a judgement about how much they are likely to use. Take a look at how much space they give to comparable stories. Then write your own to a length which is just slightly longer, giving them an opportunity to cut just a little.

Write in clear English

This ought to be obvious, but some press releases still read as though they were written in code. This is especially true of press releases written about technical subjects such as engineering, electronics or computers.

Two points need to be made here. First, technical publications will want press releases that provide technical details of products. But you still have an obligation to provide those details to the editor in plain and comprehensible English.

You also need to make a judgement about which technical terms the editor will understand and which might need explanation within the release. This will largely depend on the publication to which you are sending the release. Again, the best way to decide about this is to study the publications you are planning to hit with your press release in order to gauge the technical level at which the stories are written.

The second point is that you should not send the same kind of release to those publications which are not interested in the technical details. Perhaps a business-related publication might be interested in a story about a new product, but it will want a different kind of story to the one you send to a technical publication. The business publication will be more interested in applications and uses rather than technical details.

Beyond the use of technical terms lies the question of jargon. Every specialised business has its jargon, and it might sometimes be acceptable to use a jargon term, but you should consciously try to keep jargon to a minimum when writing for any newspaper or magazine, even a technical publication, and expunge it completely when writing about a technical or semi-technical subject for a more general publication.

Another point about clear English. A press release is not a literary work, but a working document designed to convey information from one person to another. So there is no need to write in a literary or, even worse, mock-literary style. Still more, you should avoid attempts to be 'humorous' — this practically never comes off in press releases, and sometimes kills what would otherwise be an acceptable story.

Avoid errors of grammar, spelling and punctuation

Too many press releases are spotted with the kind of elementary grammatical, spelling or punctuation mistakes that would shame a schoolboy or girl. You need to get it right, because nothing undermines the confidence of a sub-editor more than to see a piece of copy that seems to have been written by somebody who doesn't know the basics of his business.

If your English is a little shaky, make some efforts to strengthen your weak points before you start to write regular press releases. Some useful books to help are listed under Further Reading at the end of this book.

Here are some of the most common English errors in press releases with suggestions about how to avoid them:

Mixing single and plural
For example: 'The company's finance committee has decided to hold an emergency meeting and they will meet on Thursday.'

The verb 'has' rightly identifies the 'committee' as singular. But then the 'they' suggests the committee is plural. Either 'has' should be 'have' or 'they' should be 'it'.

Remedy: When you refer to any corporate body, such as a company, department or committee, decide whether you want to treat it as singular or plural — most publications prefer singular. Then ensure all verbs and pronouns referring to it are consistent.

Wrong possessive
All corporate bodies are impersonal. So they should not be referred to by personal pronouns. Biggest mistake is to use 'who' instead of 'which'. For example:

'All the company's departments, who are located at Anytown, will be involved in the expansion programme.'

Remedy: The 'who' should be replaced by 'which'. Remember that only people (and sometimes animals) attract the privilege of being called 'who'.

Muddled timings
This generally manifests itself in confusion over tenses. For example:

'Gobble and Belch has launched a new range of baby foods called Instant Gourmet. The range will be available through most supermarkets.'

Remedy: The problem here is the past 'has launched' with the future 'will be available'. It raises the question of whether the range is currently available in supermarkets, and would certainly involve an irritating and unnecessary check by a conscientious sub-editor.

The release's author should have written: 'The range is available through most supermarkets.' You should always check that the tenses you use accurately reflect the current status of what is happening.

Officialese
You may think that your press release sounds more important if you encrust it with official sounding words and portentous phrases. But editors are trained to see through them all when looking for a story. The strongest stories are always told in clear and simple English.

Officialese sounds like this:

'Objective consideration of contemporary phenomena compels the conclusion that success or failure in competitive activities exhibits no tendency to be commensurate with innate capacity, but that a considerable element of the unpredictable must inevitably be taken into account.'

George Orwell wrote the above in order to show how it is possible to garble even the most exquisitely written and clearly expressed English. The original from the King James Bible, Book of Ecclesiastes, reads:

'I returned and saw under the sun, that the race is not to the swift, nor the battle to the strong, neither yet bread to the wise, nor yet riches to men of understanding, nor yet favour to men of skill; but time and chance happeneth to them all.'

● *Action point:* Rewrite the following paragraph in clear English and compare your version with the one at the end of this chapter: 'The directors have arrived at an optimistic view of sales potential in the prevailing market conditions and have sanctioned additional capital investment in a green-field manufacturing facility.'

Avoid lawyer-speak
Sometimes, the company lawyers like to get their hands on a press release before it is issued. This is quite understandable when important legal issues, such as mergers and acquisitions, patent disputes or contracts are at stake. Certainly take their advice about the legal implications of what you are saying and about the dangers of using certain words and phrases, but don't let them rewrite the release in legalese.

Use short words when they do the job best
For example use 'say' instead of 'communicate', 'let' for 'allow', 'make' for 'manufacture', 'about' for 'approximately'. But if you use a short word, make certain it means the same as the long word. For example, 'demonstrate' and 'show' can have different meanings.

Keep clichés under control
As Samuel Goldman said: 'Let's get some new clichés.' Everyone uses a cliché from time to time. (I wouldn't care to have this book minutely examined.) However, you should take care to ensure that the clichés don't run out of control. And when you spot a cliché, replace it with a straight-forward phrase.

Leave out words that do no work
Too many press releases are packed with verbiage just for the sake of it. Each word in your release should be taking the story forward. Lazy words include 'actually', 'really', 'simply'.

Avoid the common mistakes that make a release look amateur
Some of the common ones are:

● Repetition: only say it once. If you have said it is a 'new product' in the first paragraph, you don't need to call it a 'new product' every time you refer to it.

● Extra capitals: use capitals only for proper nouns. Do not use capital letters for company positions. For example, write managing director, not Managing Director. And never write the company name all in capital letters — this irritates sub-editors who have to mark it down to lower case.

● Sideheads: a press release rarely needs sideheads, certainly not the kind of sideheads used mostly in tabloid newspapers. However, a sidehead may be acceptable where it introduces a clearly definable new section of the press release — for example, another product.

For further tips on using good English see *Mastering Business English* by Michael Bennie, especially Chapter 7 on grammar.

QUOTE . . . UNQUOTE

A press release can invariably be strengthened with a quotation, or 'quote' as journalists more sparingly call them. A quote introduces a human element into a story. Yet too many quotes in press releases read as though they have been spoken by robots.

Worse still, too many quotes read as if they haven't been spoken at all. There is a distinct whiff of the midnight oil and the committee compromise about some quotes. And worst of all, too many quotes are just paeans of praise or expressions of pious and unfulfilled hopes.

You should certainly include quotes in your press release, but make them sound natural. Follow these guidelines:

Make it human
Write the quote as though it were spoken by a normal human being talking

in a natural way. Use 'I' and 'we' and verbal contractions such as 'don't' and 'can't'. For example:

Wrong: 'Forward projections indicate a profit above those achieved in previous years.'

Right: 'I think we will make a record profit.'

Add value to the story

Make the quote provide something extra for the story. Don't just repeat in quotation marks something you have already written. For example:

Wrong: The 200 orders received in May make it the best month so far. Mr John Smith, managing director, said: 'We are delighted to have received 200 orders in May.'

Right: The 200 orders received in May make it the best month so far. Mr John Smith, managing director, said: 'We were surprised. In previous Mays, orders have gone down rather than up.'

Avoid self-congratulation

It just sounds pompous and self-serving, adds nothing to your release, and won't get used. For example:

Wrong: 'We are convinced our new widget is the finest ever manufactured,' said Mr John Smith, managing director.

Right: 'The Widget Manufacturing Association has awarded our new model its special commendation,' said Mr John Smith, managing director.

Question and answer

Question: What if the managing director or other senior manager insists on writing his own quotes and they sound awful?

Answer: Try the light-hearted approach. Ask him if he really speaks like that. Tactfully suggest he will sound more relaxed and human if the quote is reworded in more colloquial English.

A TOUCH OF THE RED PENCIL

You have drafted your press release. You have followed all the suggestions mentioned in this book. You think it reads well. Beware of self-satisfaction. Errors lurk in work you are delighted with.

Whenever possible, you should look again at your release about a day after you first drafted it. Go through it carefully to see if any editing is needed. Especially look out for:

- Ambiguity. Is everything perfectly clear? Could any statement be taken two ways?

- Grammar. Have any grammatical errors crept in? Check back with the common errors mentioned earlier in this chapter.

- Accuracy. Are all the facts and figures correct? Be positively sure they are correct — don't just think they are right.

- Repetition. Have you written the release as concisely as possible? Can you edit it down more tightly? What words can you cut out without losing any meaning?

- Story-line. Does the story-line you have written work well? Have you included all the facts needed to support it?

- Proofed. Have you read the release thoroughly for typing, spelling and punctuation errors?

Ideally, you will have somebody to help you with the editing of your press releases. A second eye often spots errors that the first eye missed. But if there is nobody available, you will have to edit your own releases. Actively look for mistakes as you do it rather than assuming everything must be right just because you wrote it.

DISTRIBUTING THE PRESS RELEASE

'The medium is the message', said communications guru Marshall McLuhan. There is more than a grain of truth to that in press releases. When your press release arrives in a newspaper or magazine office, you want it to convey both a sense of professionalism and urgency. So how you distribute the release is important.

The medium of your release can give quite the wrong impression. For example, one public relations consultant used to distribute several releases from different clients in the same envelope by second-class post. What is that saying to the editor who receives it? 'Here is a job lot of press releases. They're not that urgent because they've been in the post for three days. Nothing stands out because I've lumped them all together. Perhaps you'd like to rummage among them.' Most editors will say, 'No thanks'.

You have four main options for delivering your release. These are:

- post
- messenger
- fax
- electronic mail.

   We will take a look at each option in turn.

By post
This is by far the most common method and likely to remain so for the foreseeable future. If distributing by post, follow these rules:

Envelope
White looks smartest, but brown is acceptable. There is no need to go overboard with expensive monogrammed envelopes.

   More important, use an envelope of appropriate size. For a normal release of one, two or even three or four pages, this means a common DL envelope (8 $^5/_8$ ins by 4 $^1/_4$ ins). For a release of more pages, best move up to a C5 envelope (9ins by 6 $^3/_8$ ins). For a press pack of several releases, possibly including other material, you will need a C4 envelope (12 $^3/_4$ ins by 9ins). If you are including photographs in your release, use a board-backed envelope.

Postage
Always send by first-class post. Wherever possible try to catch the earliest post of the day to increase the chances of the release being delivered the following day. If you are sending your release overseas, use airmail.

By messenger
This is a useful option if you want to be absolutely certain of your release reaching a news office within a few hours. Within London, some of the companies that publish media directories also provide a distribution service. Details are on page 51.

   Alternatively, you can use a motor cycle courier or one of the package distribution companies. In general, it is only worth using a messenger when you are sending a package of material that cannot be conveniently faxed — for example some releases, brochures and photographs.

By fax
In theory, the fax provides the ideal medium for getting a press release quickly into the hands of an editor. In practice, faxing releases should be done sparingly and only for those stories that really do need to be in a journalist's hands within minutes.

Given the thousands of press releases issued in a typical working day, newspapers and magazines will not take too kindly to their fax machines being tied up for hours receiving press releases of minimal importance.

If you want to send your releases by fax, you should check with the editor or news editor first that he would like to receive them that way. Perhaps you will be able to agree some ground-rules about when and when not you will send him releases by fax — for example, when a story would otherwise miss his deadline.

By electronic mail
You will definitely need to discuss this with an editor before sending releases. Apart from the question of whether he wants to receive releases from you across a computer-communications network, there will also be technical issues of compatibility and security to discuss, especially if you send your releases as e-mail attachments. However, if the editor takes a significant number of stories from you, this is an option that would be worth considering.

Action points: suggested answers

Short sentences
'Writing a Press Release' is published this week by How To Books of Oxford. Peter Bartram, an author and journalist, has written 19 other books and 2,500 magazine articles.

Clear emphasis
'The directors believe sales will go up and plan to invest in a new factory.'

Final thought: the press release wot I wrote
It's a sad fact that standards of written and spoken English seem to be falling. Teachers play down the importance of grammar, spelling and punctuation in favour of 'free expression'. We won't have any of that in press releases, thank you very much. Words are the tools of a journalist's trade and your typical journalist does not like to see the language used in a slovenly way. If you feel your English is a little suspect, you should take steps to remedy your weaknesses — and get somebody to check releases until you are confident.

7
Picture Power

'Photography is truth.' — Jean-Luc Godard, *Le Petit Soldat*.

Which is not to suggest, of course, that your press release is lies. But a picture — often a photograph, sometimes an illustration or diagram — can often strengthen the story you plan to issue. In fact, sometimes a good picture will increase the chances of an otherwise average story making it into print.

IDENTIFYING TARGETS FOR PICTURES

As with your press releases, the first task is to identify those publications which accept contributed pictures or other illustrated matter. You have already identified the publications on your circulation list (see Chapter 3). Now you need to analyse their picture content.

The first question to ask is: does this publication accept contributed pictures? You may be surprised to learn that practically all publications — even national newspapers, even national TV news networks — accept contributed pictures at some time. For example, if you are a company which is a household name, a national newspaper and probably a TV news organisation will want a picture of your chairman. In some cases, it might want to take the picture itself. But it will almost certainly accept a good quality photograph for its picture library. Even if your company is not a household name, there will be plenty of opportunities to place good quality pictures.

Go through two or three back issues of your target publications and look at the kind of pictures they use. You can analyse them with the help of the checklist below. Make a note against each of your target publications as to which kind of photographs it uses.

Checklist 1
Common types of contributed photographs used by newspapers and magazines:

- mug shots (people's head and shoulders)
- products photographed in studio
- products photographed in use
- company locations (*ie* offices, shops, factory, etc)
- customer sites (especially when products installed)
- contract signing
- events (*ie* opening of offices, Royal visit, etc)
- presentation (*ie* of certificates to trainees, gold watch to pensioner)
- conference (of manager speaking at it)
- staff activity (taking part in marathon, helping at carnival, etc.)

You should also think about other kinds of illustrations which some publications might want to publish. The next checklist describes some of the other illustration opportunities. Again, you should analyse your target publications to see which kinds of illustrations are used.

Checklist 2
Some types of contributed illustrative matter used by newspapers and magazines:

- graphs
- charts
- technical drawings
- cartoons
- artists' impressions (of new buildings, new products, etc)
- maps
- logos

By the time you have been through both these checklists, you should have a comprehensive view of which kinds of illustrations will be used by which publications. There is one other point to cover. Does each publication carry its illustrations in mono (black and white) or colour? The question applies both to photographs and other illustrative matter. Having an answer to this question will help you to plan the kind of material to submit.

PROBLEM AND REMEDY
Problem: We'd like to submit more photographs to publications but simply can't afford the costs. Photographers seem to be too expensive.
Remedy: In practice, photographers' charges tend to vary widely and

the most costly are not always the best. Your best bet is to find a local photographer with press experience. In general you should not need to pay more than £75.00 an hour (1999 prices) for attendance at a photography session — or 'shoot'. In addition, photographers generally charge for travelling, film and processing.

Action point
Have you considered what might make good newsworthy material in your company? Discuss this with your colleagues. Draw up a list of possible pictures that you can use with future press releases.

WHEN TO SEND A PICTURE

Using pictures can strengthen a press relations campaign, but also adds to the cost. In order to keep your budget under control and gain the best value for money, you need to identify those opportunities when sending a picture could yield better results.

One answer to this conundrum is to send a picture when it is likely to increase the chances of gaining coverage. Let us look at a number of typical cases.

Case 1: the 'people column'
The newspaper runs a 'people column' of new appointments, often with pictures next to the items, but not always. When should you send a picture? You could send a picture with every release, but that might prove expensive. Instead, look at the picture stories in the column more closely. Is there a pattern to the pictures which are used? Possibly the items with pictures are the more senior managers mentioned in the column. So limit a picture to those occasions when you have an announcement about a senior manager.

Case 2: several pages of 'product news'
The magazine runs several pages of product news. Again, only some items carry pictures. Should you send one? In this instance, you need to look closely at the style of the product pictures the editor prefers. Are they colour or black and white (or perhaps both)? Does he prefer a studio shot with a plain background, or does he prefer a picture of the product being used? Try to narrow down exactly what it is the editor wants from a product shot, and then provide a picture which meets those specifications when you have a product announcement of sufficient importance to warrant it.

Case 3: the 'financial news' page
A trade paper runs a financial news page where it reports results from leading companies in the industry. You want to increase the impact you make with your announcement on the page. One way to do this is to provide a chart — probably a bar chart — showing how your company's turnover or profit (or both) have performed over the past, say, five years. The editor may appreciate a relevant illustration to brighten up what is often a dull looking page.

Case 4: the local paper
Your company is planning to enter a float in the local carnival. The float will be, say, a tableau of kings and queens through the ages. You can send a picture of your employees dressed in their costumes to the local paper the week before the carnival takes place. This is far more likely to make the paper, than a picture sent after the event when the paper will probably have its own pictures of the carnival.

Some general rules
As you can see, these examples boil down to a few general rules about when to send a picture:

- When the publication actively uses that kind of picture.
- When the picture adds value to the press release.
- When it is a picture story (for example, the carnival story).
- When a picture enhances the chances of the story being used.

Question and answer
Question: We've used photographers before but they never seem to come up with the pictures we really want.

Answer: Perhaps you have not briefed the photographer carefully enough. Use the briefing notes in Figure 9. Attend the shoot with the photographer. Make sure he takes the pictures you want — you are paying his bill — but be guided by any helpful suggestions that an experienced photographer will make.

WHAT MAKES A GOOD NEWSPAPER PICTURE?

Journalist Anthony Delano wrote this: 'Two kinds of photographs make unforgettable news pictures. The one where the photographer has encapsulated the quintessential split-second movement; eye and shutter finger perfectly co-ordinated by reflexes as sure as the camera mechanism

PICTURE BRIEFING

Briefing from _

Contact address _

Contact phone _

Photographer's name _

Location of shoot _

Date _

Time _

Contact at shoot _

Pictures required _

Colour or black & white _

Prints, negatives, transparencies? _ _ _ _ _ _ _ _ _ _ _ _ _ _

For use in _

Subject _

_ _

Must shots _

_ _

Other desirable shots _

_ _

Any special instructions _ _ _ _ _ _ _ _ _ _ _ _ _ _ _ _ _ _ _

Send pictures to _

Deadline _

Fee and expenses _

Fig. 9. A briefing sheet for a photographer.

itself. . . The other is taken when a picture that is an eloquent story in itself forms in the photographer's mind long before the elements of the final image come together in his patient viewfinder.'

An example in the first category is almost any great sports shot — when the photographer captures the ball sliding into the back of the net or the bail falling to the ground.

A classic example in the second category was a picture published in the *Daily Mail* following the failed attempt to extradite great train robber Ronnie Biggs from Brazil. The picture showed Superintendent Jack Slipper of Scotland Yard, who had flown to Brazil to arrest Biggs, asleep next to an empty seat. The implication was that this was the seat meant for Biggs. In fact, the seat was occupied by Slipper's assistant. He had just gone to the lavatory. The picture brilliantly summed up the story but, of course, at its heart was a lie.

A picture that tells a story

You can take a leaf from the great Fleet Street photographers and look for the picture that tells the story. A picture that tells the story is a picture which shows what is happening. Yet it is not a gimmick — where something irrelevant is brought into the picture to liven up an otherwise boring photo. On the whole, you should avoid 'gimmick' pictures because they look contrived. But creative pictures which help to tell the story are another matter. Some examples:

● Your company signs a big contract in the US. *Picture:* Not the boring hand-shaking managers, which most editors hate. Instead, the sales person who won the order hauling the Stars and Stripes up the company flagpole.

● Your company launches its smallest ever microchip (or smallest anything else). *Picture:* the microchip with a pin or a stamp or anything else which gives an example of its scale.

● A member of staff gains a professional qualification. *Picture:* the manager hanging his diploma on his office wall.

● You move to new offices. *Picture:* the managing director helping to unload the removal van.

● You raise £1,000 for charity. *Picture:* the chief fund raiser handing over a giant cheque to the charity.

- The one-millionth widget comes off the production line. *Picture:* workers crack a bottle of champagne as the widget garlanded in festive ribbon rolls by.

Action point

How could you develop some creative picture ideas for your company and its products? Organise a brain-storming session of those people concerned with the press campaign. Make a list of as many ideas as possible. Then focus on the ideas that really look like feasible news photos.

The quick guide to looking good in pictures

Nothing makes a worse picture than people glaring at the camera because they don't want to be photographed. The camera tends to magnify people's attitudes which reveals the reluctant subject to anyone who might care to glance at the picture.

You can help your staff to 'perform' better in pictures, and perhaps put them more at ease, by giving them these simple guidelines:

- Be cooperative. The photographer wants to take the best possible picture of you. He may need to move some furniture, close the curtains, or clear clutter on your desk. Don't object — he is trying to help you.

- Help with location. The photographer may want to take a picture out of the office. Help him by suggesting suitable places with an interesting backdrop — in the factory, elsewhere on your company site or in the local town.

- Look the part. Men: Straighten your tie. Button your jacket. Women: Adjust your make-up. Both: Check your hair.

- Avoid an audience. Keep wise-cracking office colleagues off the shoot. It makes the subject of the picture ill at ease.

- Animate your face. For example, by talking. But don't pull odd expressions. Keep face muscles relaxed.

- Don't be rigid. Or adopt an awkward posture. Feel natural and you will look natural.

- In groups, stand close together. It may feel odd, but won't look it. It will make a 'tight' picture which editors prefer.

- Relax and enjoy. Then people who see the picture will say: 'That's a good one of you.'

Checklist: 10 traps to avoid in PR photographs
- Large unposed groups.
- Large posed groups.
- People pulling faces because they think it's funny.
- The boss's secretary pretending to be a top model.
- Outside shot of the offices with no-one around.
- Inside shot of the offices with staff bored, eating sandwiches, etc.
- Untidy offices.
- Offices that have been tidied so much they look as though no work is ever done there.
- Semi-clothed models draped over unlikely products.
- Any picture of the firm's Christmas party.

Question and answer
Question: What can I do when it's important to have a picture of a manager to support a press release, but the manager simply won't play ball?

Answer: The root of the problem is often that he is afraid of 'looking a fool' at the shoot. Reassure him by pointing out that only he, you and the photographer will be present. Give him the chance to choose the picture which is used. (But don't let him choose a totally unsuitable one.)

A NOTE ON THE TECHNICALITIES

Any picture you send to a newspaper or magazine must be of sufficient quality to reproduce well. Yet newspapers and magazines still receive pictures of people which appear to have been taken in a railway station photo-booth. There are different technical requirements for black and white and colour pictures.

Black and white
If the picture is heading for a paper printed on newsprint it needs strong contrasts between the blacks and whites. A newspaper picture is printed at fairly low quality in which the whites become less white and blacks less black. The printing process actually reduces the contrast in the picture. So you need to make sure there is plenty of contrast to start with.

For a magazine picture, or any picture printed in a publication with coated (glossy) paper, the contrast is slightly less important. The picture will be printed to higher technical standards which will retain most of the original contrast. Even so, it pays to send a picture with good contrast as it makes a more effective shot.

There is no 'right' size for a newspaper picture. But because the picture needs to be conveniently handled, it should not be too small — certainly not less than about 6 ins by 4 ins. If a picture is to be used at a large size, then the print you send can do with being larger. When a picture is blown up substantially some of the sharpness can be lost.

Colour

In general, editors prefer colour transparencies to colour prints as they produce a rather higher quality result in the printed newspaper or magazine. In most cases a 35mm transparency is quite acceptable, providing it is sharply in focus. Unfortunately too many are not. But for higher quality — and easier handling by the picture editor — a 2 $\frac{1}{4}$ ins transparency is better. On rare occasions, where a picture is to be reproduced in a large size at high quality, one of the specialist larger sizes of transparency will produce the best results. Your photographer will advise on the best size to produce.

Care of pictures

Too many pictures turn up on editors' desks already so badly damaged they are unusable. The point to start caring for your pictures is in your own office. You need to set up a proper filing system for your pictures in which both prints and their negatives and transparencies are filed in clearly labelled envelopes. But do not write on the envelopes while pictures are in it as they can become scratched or dented.

In order to make your pictures readily accessible it pays to build a working photofile containing photocopies of your prints and simple black and white 'positionals' of your transparencies. (Your photographer can provide the positionals.)

The pictures in your photofile can be labelled with captions and dates, mounted on sheets and held in a ring binder. You should cross reference each sheet of pictures to the originals in your filing system. In this way, you can easily locate the picture you want without handling, and possibly damaging, the originals.

Pictures often become damaged by careless handling, so here are some rules to follow:

- Never write on the back of pictures.
- Never fix them to each other or a letter with paper clips or staples.
- Don't keep them in piles of other papers — you might write on them accidentally,
- Store them in cellophane bags or envelopes, not pressed too tightly together.

Finally, pictures become damaged in transit. Always send black and white prints in board-backed envelopes and transparencies in jiffy bags. But especially avoid transparencies with glass coverings as the glass always seems to shatter into lethal fragments no matter how thick the jiffy bag.

Action point

Start keeping a simple photo library of the pictures you might need regularly. Picture library shots would include your most senior managers, especially your chairman and managing director, and main products. Draw up a list of the pictures you ought to have in your organisation's picture library.

EFFECTIVE CAPTION WRITING

The first purpose of a picture caption is to inform, the second to encourage the reader to look at the story. You should approach the writing of captions with those two points firmly in mind.

Informing the reader

First, if the caption does not inform, it has failed. Any caption should say who or what the picture is. You need to provide a full but succinct explanation. Do not assume the editor will know what you are talking about because he has read the accompanying press release. The release and the picture may be separated and handled by different people in the newspaper office.

So, for example, these captions are all wrong.

John Smith

Gobble and Belch's new head office

The PC2000

They fail because they do not provide enough information for the reader to understand the full context. Who is John Smith? What is the PC2000? Better versions are:

John Smith, managing director of Gobble and Belch.

Gobble and Belch's new head office at 17 High Road, Anytown.

The PC2000 personal computer, launched on July 10th by Megatechnologies.

Take care to caption pictures accurately. For example, confusion often arises in a caption of a picture with several people in it. List the names starting from the left (and say so in the caption) with name first and position after, separating each individual with a semi-colon. For example:
'Picture shows (from left) John Smith, managing director of Gobble and Belch; Ted Jones, marketing director; Len Taylor, production director; and Councillor Freda Davis, Mayor of Anytown.'
The caption is perfectly clear with no room for confusion.

Encouraging the reader

A good caption in a newspaper or magazine encourages the reader to dip into the story. There is no reason why you should not use the same technique. After all, you will normally send a picture with a release and the picture often catches the editor's eye first.

One way to do this is to link the caption specifically to the story in such a way that the editor will want to use the story and picture together. For example, you can introduce emotion into the caption. Such as:

Delighted: John Smith, managing director of Gobble and Belch, after winning the £1m contract.

This has a powerful word — delighted — to kick off the caption and this relates the picture specifically to the news story. In other words, this isn't any old picture of John Smith. This is a specific picture of John Smith taken after winning the contract. (Of course, the picture must be taken after the contract victory and John Smith should look delighted.) The caption has reinforced the picture, the picture has reinforced the story and both stand a greater chance of being used.

Another approach is to pull a telling quote out of the story and add it to the caption. For example:

> Gobble and Belch managing director John Smith: 'Babies have a taste for the high life'.

In this example, you need to place the description of John Smith before his name to make the caption work. Alternatively, you can handle the caption this way:

> John Smith, managing director of Gobble and Belch, said: 'Babies have a taste for the high life.'

The picture story
Occasionally, you may want to send out a release where the picture is the main element of the story. In this case, you can attach a longer caption to the picture to create a picture story.

If you do this, however, you must first make certain that the picture you have is strong enough to run as a picture story. It needs to be the kind of picture that an editor would want to publish on its own merits. Then you must make certain that the story can conveniently be summed up in a few short sentences. For example:

> QUADS HAVE BIRTHDAY TREAT
>
> Abigail, Barry, Clarissa and Danny (from left) tuck into a treat, Smoked Salmon and Caviar, one of the Gourmet Foods' range from Gobble and Belch. The quads ate their fill before blowing out the candle on their first birthday cake. Their mum and dad, Mr and Mrs Tom Brown, of Low Road, Anytown, served up the meal to their growing foursome.

The picture tells the story and the words are there to supply the detail.

Caption technicalities
With black and white photographs, the caption should be typed or word-processed onto sheets of paper which are then stuck with sellotape on to the back of the picture. Don't use sticky labels as the editor may want to

detach the caption from the picture for editing. And certainly do not write on the back of the picture.

In the case of colour transparencies, you should stick a small label with the main subject on to the transparency mounting. One effective way to send the transparency is in an envelope with the full caption on a sheet of paper in the envelope.

Every caption should contain the same contact information as a press release: the name and address of the sender together with day time and (if appropriate) night time telephone numbers.

Finally, it is not normal to ask publications to return pictures when sent on spec. However, if you supply a picture at a publication's request, there is no reason why you should not ask them to send it back to you when they have finished with it.

Final thought: not one for the album

More money is probably wasted in photography than in any other single public relations activity. Why? Too many press officers have a completely unrealistic view of the kinds of pictures a newspaper or magazine will want to publish. As a result, photographers are hired to snap off rolls of film that will never be used in print. It may flatter the ego of the managers and others who preen themselves before the camera — but it takes your press relations campaign nowhere. Understand what photographs each newspaper or magazine you deal with is likely to publish. Only provide those pictures. In fact, build a reputation for supplying the kind of pictures a magazine wants. Soon the editor will be asking you for more. Remember: in a press relations campaign, the purpose of taking a picture is to have it published, not mounted in an album.

8
Making News

'Journalism largely consists of saying "Lord Jones is dead" to people who never knew Lord Jones was alive.' — G.K. Chesterton.

Well, partly. But, as we have already seen, most journalism rides on identifying the subjects and issues which the paying customer wants to read about. If your press releases do this, too, you will win many column inches of coverage for your company or organisation.

GIVING A PRESS RELEASE MORE CLOUT

Is there anything you can do to increase the chance of an editor using your release? There are a number of things you can consider, but it is only fair to say that we are entering territory here where there are no clear-cut answers. So the ideas mentioned below need to be used skilfully and with care.

Provide an exclusive

Your story might stand more chance of making it into at least one publication if you provide it as an exclusive. Editors naturally like to run stories that no other publication has, especially competing publications. If you think this might be worth considering, you must think carefully about a number of issues.

First, the story needs to be 'exclusive' material. If it is a middle ranking story that might make a few column inches on a quiet day, then few editors will become excited by the offer of an exclusive. On the other hand, the offer of an exclusive might just tip the balance between rejection and acceptance. You need to make a fine judgement, based largely on what you know about the editor's news values.

In the second instance, you have a story that is definitely hot. Almost certainly several publications, perhaps the newspapers and magazines serving your industry, will run it. Should you offer it to one and not the others? The case for doing so is that the one that gets it might splash the story more extensively than if it was just one of several publications running the same story.

The case against is that you could annoy the editors of the other publications. This is a difficult question to resolve and, again, partly rests on how much you know about the news values of the editors involved. Perhaps you know that one editor is especially interested in this topic, while the editor of the rival paper is not so enthusiastic. That could be a case for giving the keen editor the story as an exclusive.

Over a period of time, you should keep all the editors satisfied providing you treat them in an even handed way. Don't, for example, give all your exclusives to the same editor. Above all, avoid giving the impression that you are trying to play one editor off against another. In that way, you are certain to lose the goodwill of both. Editors are wise in the ways of newspapers and know that sometimes a rival publication will get a story they don't have, and that on other occasions the reverse will be true. They will live with this providing you play the game too and are open and honest in your dealings with them.

Write a letter

Do you need to write an accompanying letter with your press release? In 99 out of 100 cases the answer is no. (And there is no need to send a compliments slip, either.) In the hundredth case, a letter might just enhance the release's chances of making its way into print.

But the letter needs to be more than a note saying you are enclosing a press release. You might, for example, add information about the reason you are sending it. Perhaps you are asking whether the editor would like the story as an exclusive. Alternatively, you might be offering a demonstration of the product mentioned in the release. Or an interview with the subject of the story, perhaps a newly appointed managing director.

The key point about a letter is this: does it add anything useful to the information in the release? If not, don't send one.

Telephone the journalist

The ground rules here are similar for letter writing. Telephone if you have something extra to add. In fact, if you are going to telephone it is often better to do so before sending the release. You can then establish whether the story will be of value and whether what you have to offer is of interest.

But at this point a giant warning must be inserted. Busy journalists are bombarded with telephone calls all day long. Too many of the calls are from time-wasters. These are the calls not to make:

'Have you received our press release?'

'Could you send us a press cutting if you use it?'

'We've advertised in (are thinking of advertising in) your magazine and wonder if you'd be interested in writing about us?'

If you plan to telephone a journalist, make your call as efficient and business-like as possible by following the guidelines in the checklist below.

Checklist: How to telephone a journalist
- Know the right journalist to speak to for the story you have.
- Ask for the journalist by name.
- Explain who you are and where you are from.
- Get straight to the point about what you have to offer.
- Have background information to hand so you can answer queries on the spot.
- Anticipate questions and have your answers ready.
- Don't argue if the journalist says he's not interested.
- Try to ring at a non-busy time (not on 'press day').

Be available to take queries

Imagine this scenario: you have sent out your press release. It has genuine news value and a number of newspapers and magazines want to run the story, each giving it its own 'spin'. To do so, they want more information from you. That almost certainly involves talking to senior managers over the phone.

But the journalists call, and they get one of these answers:

'He's in a meeting.'

'He's on holiday.'

'He's out of the office today.'

'He doesn't take calls from journalists.'

'Tell me what it's about, and I'll decide whether to put you through.'

'Is it important?'

The failure to be available is probably the biggest single cause of killing those stories that could have made it into the papers. The rule you must follow is this: if you send out a release be certain that the contact named on it will be available on the days the journalists are likely to ring. Generally, this will be on the day they receive the release or within two or three days of it — although you could receive calls from monthly magazines a week or two afterwards.

No-one expects a senior manager to be kicking his heels in the office waiting for calls from journalists. But you need to set up machinery to ensure that he can be contacted quickly if needed for a press comment, especially on the day when you are likely to get most of the calls.

Even being available is not quite enough. You need to anticipate the kind of questions that your release might raise. (Of course, if those questions are sufficiently important, the answers should be included in the story.) But journalists will often want that little bit more not in the release so they can personalise a story. You should make sure you have covered most of the areas they are likely to ask about and that the manager who will take the calls has the information readily to hand.

Not everyone can be in the office all the time. Make sure that the switchboard knows that journalists may be calling and that they pass on messages promptly. That means within half an hour of getting them. Then call back as soon as possible. The journalist may be sitting on a deadline and waiting for your call.

Add a freebie

Here we move into dangerous territory. There was a time when it was not too unusual to receive some kind of promotional gift with a press release. Often the gift was a calendar or diary or some equally inoffensive item, usually sent around Christmas. But it was not unknown to receive a bottle of Scotch, a fine Stilton cheese or even a case of wine.

There are certainly dangers in sending out that kind of gift. No journalist likes to feel he is being 'bought'. On the other hand, there are no known examples of a journalist returning a free case of wine.

The best advice is not to send gifts that have any significant monetary value. The diaries, calendars, company pens and so on are unlikely to cause offence. But, then, they are unlikely to do much for you, either.

It is best to stick to sending the most newsworthy press releases you can write.

GETTING TO KNOW A JOURNALIST

As you develop a press relations campaign, it is likely that you will come to know a few journalists. Most organisations find there is a core of publications and journalists who are regularly interested in what they have to offer, while a wider audience may take a story less often.

If you develop the right kind of relationship with those journalists most interested in your organisation, you will find it easier to place stories. But what is the right kind of relationship?

Three pillars of good relations

Essentially, the best kind of relationship between a press officer and a journalist is based on three pillars.

It is based on trust

You should never do anything that might make a journalist doubt the reliability of the information you are sending him. Of course, you will never do anything as crass as tell a direct lie (although people do). But, too often, the 'facts' in press releases bend rather too far from the truth, the whole truth and nothing but the truth.

Products which have been 'launched' but which on further enquiry are 'not quite ready', 'users' who haven't quite installed the system, 'sales' which haven't quite reached the figure given. There may be a short term advantage in bending the facts. But there is only long term disaster. Once a journalist finds that the information you provide is not reliable, he will not take on trust anything you tell him — even your own name.

It is based on openness

You will find that as you build a relationship of trust with a journalist he will be more open with you. He may tell you more about the kinds of stories he particularly wants, the type of information you could help with. He may tip you off about future feature articles, special surveys and the like.

You, too, can afford to be more open about the kind of news opportunities you might have in the future. You can also help with more background information so that he understands the context of your organisation and its activities better. Yet bear in mind this caveat: a journalist's first loyalty is to his newspaper. If he gets a story, he will publish it. So while openness is healthy, it also pays to be prudent about what you say, especially in informal situations.

It is based on reliability

To a journalist, the world is full of inept PR people who provide the wrong information too late or not at all. To a press officer, the world is full of incompetent journalists, who can't spell a name right or get two simple facts in the correct order. Of course, it is not like that, but sometimes it seems like it.

If you are a press officer, make sure you provide reliable information as soon as possible. As we have seen, be available to answer queries. Check your facts before you provide them. You will find that if you are reliable, the journalist will be able to do a better job in writing about your company.

An entertaining question

Finally, what about the vexed question of entertaining journalists? When should you invite them out to lunch? What should you offer if they visit your offices? Should you always buy the drinks?

The first point is that you can't buy good copy with gin and tonics. There are still PR people who think the best way to make the news pages is via a four course lunch at the Ritz. And, let it be said, there are still plenty of journalists who encourage this delusion. After all, few people turn up the chance of a hot meal.

But any good journalist wants a story first — and the meal second. Having said that, there is no reason why you should not invite a journalist to lunch if there is a reason to do so. Such reasons can include providing the background on a specific story, exploring ways in which you can provide useful information to the journalist in future, or as a keeping-in-touch meeting with a journalist you periodically supply with stories.

If it is your invitation, the journalist will generally expect you to foot the bill. If the journalist invites you, he will pay. It is as simple as that.

KEEPING OUT OF DANGER

When you write a press release, there are three main danger areas you need to be aware of. These are wrong facts, libel and copyright.

Facts are sacred

'Comment is free but facts are sacred,' is a well known quotation from C.P. Scott, one of the greatest editors of the *Manchester Guardian*. Not so well known is the sentence he used before that: 'Neither in what it [a newspaper] gives, nor in what it does not give, nor in the mode of presentation, must the unclouded face of truth suffer wrong.'

These high ideals are not achieved by modern popular newspapers, but you should aspire to them in your press releases. Facts should be checked. You should not assume they are correct because you think they are. You should know they are.

It is especially important to check facts that you have second hand — for example, figures you might see in another publication. After all, you can't believe everything you read in the papers.

Question and answer

Question: What should I do if I find an error in a press release I've already issued?

Answer: You need to correct it as rapidly as possible — preferably before it finds its way into print. You need to telephone or fax the publications you have sent it to with a correction and apology. Don't just send corrections by post. By the time they arrive the mistake may be on 10 million people's breakfast tables.

Public scandal, odium and contempt

Which is, broadly speaking, what somebody has to prove they have been brought into if they have been libelled. You must remember that you can libel companies and organisations as well as people.

Having said that, you should not find that libel is a problem in press releases given that your releases will be approved by the people mentioned in them. On the other hand, there are a couple of potential problem areas.

● If you are comparing your own product with that of a rival. The comparison needs to be accurate and honest and you need to believe that the comparison you have made is true and fair.

● If your company spokesperson — say the managing director or other senior manager — is quoted as criticising an outside body, such as the local council or a government department. Again, the criticism needs to be based on accurate facts and to be honestly made.

This is not a legal textbook, but you libel somebody if what you say:

● Tends to lower the victim in the estimation of right-thinking members of society.

● Tends to bring the victim into hatred, ridicule, contempt, dislike or disesteem with those right-thinkers.

● Tends to make the victim shunned, avoided or cut off from the said right-thinkers.

Question and answer

Question: What should we do if we become involved in a libel action?

Answer: Immediately seek the advice of a firm of solicitors that has special expertise in libel. Such firms include:

Peter Carter-Ruck & Partners, 76 Shoe Lane, London EC4A 3JB. Tel: (0171) 353 5005.

Crocker Oswald Hickson, 10 Gough Square, London EC4A 3NJ. Tel: (0171) 353 0311.

The danger of being a copycat

Like libel, **copyright** is another legal minefield. You should not run into problems when writing about your own company and its products and services. There should be no problems if you quote your organisation's own publications, unless you are quoting material that has been lifted by your company publications from somewhere else.

Anything written by other people is their copyright, unless they have assigned the copyright to somebody else, which is often the case with written material produced by companies. This means, as a general rule, you should not take material from other publications and include it in your press releases, except with permission.

However, it is possible to quote from other people's work if you are 'fair dealing' — that is quoting extracts of reasonable length for the purposes of criticism or review. In this instance, you must provide 'sufficient acknowledgement' of the original. As with libel, if you run into any difficulties with copyright, you should consult a solicitor.

Question and answer

Question: If a magazine writes a flattering article about my company or product, can I copy the article and send it to my customers?

Answer: No. The article is the copyright of the magazine. You should ask the magazine's permission before you make any large number of copies. Most publications provide a reprint service to cater for just this situation.

JUDGING THE RESULTS OF YOUR PRESS COVERAGE

How well am I doing? It is a natural question for anyone involved in press relations to ask. You have a simple way to judge: are your press releases used? If they are, then you must be doing something right. If not, perhaps you should review the advice contained in this book.

One way to get your whole organisation behind a press relations campaign is to let them see the benefits of it. Make sure that press cuttings are circulated to key managers and department heads. Keep a press cuttings book in reception.

You may also want to keep some statistics on the overall impact your press relations campaign is making. There are three main ways in which you can measure the impact of your coverage without incurring great expense:

- **Column inches**: this is a crude measure, but it provides a warm feeling if there are plenty of cuttings. But not all coverage carries the same weight or is of the same value. Some coverage may actually be harmful. Some of it may not be as a result of your press releases. So perhaps column inches is too crude a measure for you.

- **Weighted measurement**: this is a couple of steps up from measuring the column inches. You weight each cutting according to its size (column inches), publication circulation (how many people it reached) and general usefulness (you must make your own subjective judgement). In doing this, you devise your own points scheme which reflects your own objectives and concerns.

- **Audience-related measurement**: This is a way of measuring the impact the coverage has made with your target audiences — the people you really want to influence. You measure the coverage against the likely proportion of your target audience reached by the media carrying the coverage. By collating details of the circulation profiles of publications in which material about your organisation appears and comparing that against the size of your target audience, you can get a fair measure of whether your coverage is appearing in the best possible media.

Beyond these methods, it is possible to commission market research surveys to gauge the impact of your coverage. But, of course, such exercises can prove expensive. An alternative is to have your press coverage evaluated by a specialist service. Portfolio Metrica (0171 240 4849) uses a special computer program to evaluate the value of press coverage.

Question and answer

Question: We're missing some of our cuttings because we don't see every copy of all the publications we send press releases to.

Answer: Use a press cuttings agency. They're not perfect and they miss cuttings too, but they monitor large numbers of publications. It is still useful if you keep an eye on the core publications in your distribution list. Details of some agencies are under Useful Addresses at the end of the book.

A FINAL WORD

Is it all worth it? Could your time be better spent doing something other than putting out press releases? At the end of the day, press coverage is helpful if it aids your company in achieving its business objectives. If it does that, it is a worthwhile activity.

If it doesn't, then you need to ask some fundamental questions. Is press relations an appropriate marketing tool for our organisation? If it is, are we approaching the subject in the right way?

If you decide press relations can help your organisation — and 99 times out of 100 it can — then hopefully this book has put you on the right track. Like any other business activity, you will not achieve best results if you approach press relations in a casual and unprofessional way.

But a well organised and competently implemented press campaign can deliver real business benefits.

And it's great to see yourself in print.

Final thought: the fatal attraction
Sooner or later in your career as a press officer you will come across this fatal attraction: the opportunity to con a journalist with a story which is nearly but not quite true.

Perhaps the facts have to be massaged only so slightly to make it seem like a winning story instead of an also-ran. Resist this temptation. Of course, some journalists massage the facts in some of their stories. That is their privilege and, sometimes, their undoing. They do not require any assistance from you in this dubious activity. Stick to the facts and tell them in the most compelling way possible — that is the best policy. And it pays long-term dividends.

Appendix

Marks out of ten

Now let us look at some of the theory in practice. The following pages contain real press releases — some good, some not so good — which are critically evaluated and marked out of ten.

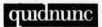

9th February 1999

"80% OF BRITISH COMPANIES SENDING MONEY UP IN FLAMES"

Most IT Projects Fall at the First Post

British companies are wasting millions of pounds each year on ill-conceived systems and are failing to turn IT into a strategic business advantage. This was the message today from one of the most innovative software consultancies in Britain, which claims that the traditional approach to specifying IT projects is failing the client.

Quidnunc, a high-quality software house known for its customers' high satisfaction ratings, has analysed the incoming specifications it has received for proposed IT projects. Over 80% are conceived in virtual isolation from the real business needs, resulting in white elephants that are avoided by end users or fail to deliver the desired improvements. According to Quidnunc, the problem unbelievably still lies in the emphasis on 'system needs' rather than on what the users are actually trying to achieve.

Quidnunc's CEO, Laurence Holt has over ten years' experience of IT project management. He commented, "The way most IT projects are specified is as good as sending money up in flames. We receive over a hundred specification documents a year from major UK companies, and most of them talk relentlessly in terms of 'the system'. When we start looking at these documents, they don't stand up to simple challenges because they're not focused on what the end user needs to do. It's like getting into a taxi and telling the cabby that your journey should be by the quickest route and that you don't want him to chat. That may be true, but what he really needs to know is where you want to go."

m.f.

126

In order to deal with this problem Quidnunc has developed a technique which distils the key business objectives of the user into 20 or 30 points. These can be prioritised, and the top ones addressed first. But more importantly perhaps, everyone involved in the project, business and IT people alike, can hold these points in their heads, ensuring everyone is speaking the same language and is focused on the same priorities. By truly capturing the business goals that users need to achieve, Quidnunc ensures that the resulting system supports the company strategy rather than perpetuating sometimes-irrelevant activities.

Holt continues, "It's a simple idea, but the impact is huge. We recently used this process to reverse a five-year history of failure in a national professional service organisation. We built the priority items within six months, and after we'd implemented it the Chief Executive said, 'You've taken away our horse and cart and given us a Ferrari.'"

ends

About Quidnunc

Quidnunc is a software consultancy whose creative approach to software, design and implementation puts it in a field of its own. Founded in 1987 by Laurence Holt, Quidnunc now employs over a hundred people, and will build £10 million worth of software this year alone. The company is head-quartered in West London, with offices in New York, Brighton, and a development facility in Bangalore, India. Quidnunc focuses on three core competencies: running projects effectively; strong software design; and growing people. By emphasising these elements, Quidnunc has delivered hundreds of successful projects, and consistently scores well above the average in customer satisfaction surveys.

For more information contact:

Clare Taylor or Giles Scott
Marbles
01491 411789
cltaylor@marbles.co.uk
http://www.marbles.co.uk

Tania Hodgkinson
Quidnunc Limited
0181 741 7117
taniah@quidnunc.com
http://www.quidnunc.com

QUIDNUNC
The sensational headline that doesn't stand up. The release doesn't provide the kind of statistical detail that is necessary to make journalists take this story seriously. How much money is going up in flames? How can they be sure the number is 80% of companies? Even the release admits this figure is based only on Quidnunc's experience.
Marks out of ten: 4

FEBRUARY 17. 1999

BT'S NEW CUSTOMER CENTRE BOOSTS BUSINESSES' COMPETITIVENESS

The UK's first BT Customer Centre to serve London and the South-East is to be opened officially on February 19 in Croydon, by the town's mayor, Councillor Pat Ryan, and BT's Group Finance Director Robert Brace. The Customer Centre lets businesses see technology in action and enables them to understand how it can help them become more competitive. With so much choice, seeing and trying equipment first is essential for many businesses.

The new Customer Centre occupiés 4,500 square feet and features a number of business environments where the latest BT products and services will be demonstrated in an interactive and informative way. The business environments are designed to track the communications and IT requirements of a business through its life cycle and encompass the following themes: *Business Flexibility at Home; Freedom with Business Mobility; Business Efficiency; Business Accessibility; Call Centre Solutions* and *Advanced Voice Services.*

There is also an environment called *Imagine*, where visitors can watch a video of today's industry commentators outlining their respective visions of how technology will have an impact on every aspect of our lives – from the business world right through to healthcare and education. These industry visionaries include Graham Whitehead, BT advanced concepts manager, Professor Colin Cornall of Henley Management College and Jan Dobson. director of creative technology at Bristol University.

In addition, the centre features videos of BT customers, from a variety of sectors, such as Solaglas. Tarmac and a teleworker, explaining how technology has impacted positively on their business practices, business efficiency and their quality of life to the extent that it is viewed not as a "competitive advantage, but as a competitive necessity".

more....

BT Corporate Relations
BT Centre 81 Newgate Street London EC1A 7AJ
British Telecommunications plc Registered Office 81 Newgate Street LONDON EC1A 7AJ Registered in England no. 1800000

128

BT'S NEW CUSTOMER CENTRE BOOSTS...(2)

Visitors to the centre will also be able to seek expert advice from five BT business solutions specialists who will be in residence to help answer specific queries from businesspeople.

Don Mildenhall, General Manager BT indirect channels, said: "Technology has become an integral part of most businesses and it can also represent a considerable investment. BT believes that it is important to assist companies in this area - this is why we have experts on hand to give help and answer specific questions and why we have the latest products and services on display for 'hands-on' demonstrations."

The new centre in Croydon is the second BT customer centre in a growing nationwide chain opening to increase business understanding of, and access, to new technology. The programme got off to a successful start last year, with the opening of the first customer centre in Birmingham's Trinity Park.

Don Mildenhall said: "For the first time, businesses are able to "test drive" technology before implementing it within their organisations. The Croydon Centre will be an asset to all businesses in the region, whether they be small businesses or large corporations."

Businesses located in Greater London and the South-East can book a visit by calling free on **0800 783 5808**. or by visiting the website at www.trinitypark.bt.com. Alternatively, customers can visit the centre by booking an appointment during opening hours. 9.00-17.30, Monday to Friday. The new BT Customer Centre is located at 85 Station Road, Croydon, CR0 2RD.

BT is planning the development of further BT customer centres at other key sites across the UK. The next site will open in Manchester in March.

- ends -

Note to editors

Cobalt. the brand and design company which created and project managed BT's Trinity Park Customer Centre. won the 1998 DBA and Marketing Week Design Effectiveness Award for their work on the Centre. *For further information or to arrange media visits please contact:*

Neil Bent. Le Fevre Communications. Tel: 01865 202666. Mobile: 07887 568930.
This news release and other media information may be accessed in the BT Communications Store. BT's on-line information resource for journalists and researchers. **http://www.commstore.bt.com** .

BT
The local story for the local papers. This story won't make much coverage outside the Croydon area. So the authors would have done better to concentrate on more local information rather than general business background. A one-pager would have been enough.
Marks out of ten: 6

Embargoed for 00:01 hours, Monday, 15 February 1999

IPD urges Government to reveal 'Full Monty' on skills shortages

Current estimates of the extent of the UK's skills gap may be false, according to the personnel and training profession, because calculation methods fail to give the full picture.

Responding to the recommendations of the first report of the national skills taskforce, the Institute of Personnel and Development (IPD) urges the government not to depend exclusively on formal qualifications as a measure of skills shortages. According to the IPD, formal qualifications only provide a partial picture of the economy's skills because so many workers acquire their skills informally.

Roy Harrison, IPD policy adviser, says: "Companies often depend on the informal acquisition of skills amongst their employees to meet immediate job needs, particularly in sectors like IT which experience particularly rapid change. Government strategies to deal with skills gaps must acknowledge that employers and their staff usually spend more time and money in on-the-job training and development than they do in formal training."

Harrison also says that any national strategy for skills shortages should start with a national audit of the skills requirements of existing jobs in the economy: "We cannot identify where we have skills shortages or skills gaps until we have made a definitive analysis of the jobs available and the skills required. Such an analysis would ensure that funding packages, intended to improve the UK's skills, are directed where they are really needed.

- more -

PD House, Camp Road, London SW19 4UX Press Office tel. 0181 263 3251/3365 fax: 0181 263 3244

"Targets to improve the level and range of skills in the UK workforce only address half the story. The supply of skills needs to respond to skill demand if we are to avoid either investing in the wrong training and development or producing large numbers of frustrated people with excellent skills but no jobs."

- The Institute of Personnel and Development (IPD) has almost 95,000 members and is the leading professional institute for those involved in the management and development of people.
- The IPD website address is http://www.ipd.co.uk

-ends-

Press enquiries: Memuna Forna,
IPD Press Office, Camp Rd, London SW19 4UX
Tel: 0181 263 3251/ Fax: 0181 263 3244

INSTITUTE OF PERSONNEL AND DEVELOPMENT
Giving a story top spin. An opinion story that taps into the title of a well-known film to give the story top spin. But the release does not pick up the headline theme in the body copy, undermining an otherwise good idea.
Marks out of ten: 7

Countrywide Residential Lettings

12th February 1999

EXPANSION FOR COUNTRYWIDE RESIDENTIAL LETTINGS
as they acquire GA Property Services' Northern Residential Lettings & Block Management Business

Countrywide Residential Lettings, one of the UK's largest specialist residential lettings and property management companies, has announced the acquisition of GA Property Services' Northern Residential Lettings, together with their national Block Management business which is to be integrated with Countrywide Property Management, a trading subsidiary.

The acquisition takes them to over 30,000 properties under management, and strengthens their High Street presence in strategic towns and cities, especially in Scotland and in the North of England, with more than 80 branches across the country.

"Residential lettings and property management is our core business, and we have been growing it year on year. There is a natural synergy with the GA network we have acquired," says Countrywide Residential Lettings Managing Director, David George FRICS. "Our regional structure of legal and property management centres linked into local branches, with a tight focus on local knowledge and expertise, means that we are able to quickly integrate the additional tenanted properties within our systems.

"Over the last year alone, we have seen significant rental rises combined with an expanding demand for good quality rented properties, especially in town and city centres. All our research indicates that the trend is continuing and our expansion provides landlords with the opportunity to draw on a unique range of professional expertise which is totally dedicated to their market.

"We will be writing to all landlords and tenants personally, but, in the meantime, they can be assured that, as part of a major public company, the high level of personal service which they have grown to expect will be sustained."

With the integration of GA's block management business, Countrywide Property Management's UK network has expanded to 13 offices. "This division is now one of the major players in a highly specialised sector, and the acquisition has given it a truly national operational base," adds Mr. George.

Countrywide Residential Lettings, with Countrywide Property Management, are part of Countrywide Assured plc. Both divisions have membership of their respective professional bodies: The Association of Residential Lettings Agents and the Association of Residential Managing Agents and are governed by strict codes of practice.

For further information, please contact:
David George, FRICS, Managing Director, Countrywide Residential Lettings
Telephone: 01702-330073

COUNTRYSIDE RESIDENTIAL LETTINGS
More facts needed. An interesting story for the property industry and the financial community. But the release needs more information on the financial background of the companies involved to make it work on the finance pages of newspapers. And the headline layout is wrong.
Marks out of ten: 6

News Release

NEW HOLIDAY BROCHURE SERVICE FOR INTERNET USERS

Co-op Travelcare Direct has launched a new Internet service, designed to deliver holiday brochures direct to the home.

More than 200 holiday brochures from over 50 operators including Cosmos, Unijet and Kuoni are now available via Co-op Travelcare's Holiday Deals website at **www.co-op-travelcare.co.uk.**

The site - one of only two operated by a major UK travel chain - includes a new brochure search facility. Users input their holiday requirements and are then presented with a selection of brochures to suit their needs.

They can put a maximum of five brochures in their on-line "shopping basket", which are then dispatched by post. Once they have made their holiday choice, they telephone Co-op Travelcare Direct to make the booking. The service is available to Internet users both in the UK and the Republic of Ireland.

Jason Edwards, Sales Development Manager for Co-op Travelcare Direct explained: "This service allows people to begin choosing their holiday at any time of the day or night from home or office. A growing number of people are using the Internet to obtain holiday information prior to booking by telephone ... we believe this service will be of great benefit to holidaymakers."

Co-op Travelcare's Holiday Deals website also offers a host of other features including access to up-to-the-minute holiday and flight bargains via its unique Bargain Basement search facility.

- ends -

For further information please contact:
Phil Edwards   **22 February 1999**
Public Relations Manager
Co-op Travelcare   Tel: 0161-827 5289

TRAVELCARE
Everything a press release should be. Informative and to the point. This is not an earth-shattering story so the writer has wisely confined it to one page. Well written in short uncomplicated sentences.
Marks out of ten: 9

Axial
Systems Limited

Subject: Automated Reporting and long term Trend Analysis
Date: 19.02.99
Contact: Claire Jenkins, Axial Systems Ltd
             Email: Claire@axial.co.uk   Tel: 01628 418000

D E S K T A L K

TREND

Intelligent Performance

As costs associated with increasingly complex networks rise, it is crucial that
administrators have a clear picture of their network's performance.
Network managers often face the problem of having insufficient visibility of their
network traffic and the applications and users that create it. This means they cannot
make accurate predictions of the future requirements for future network expansion.

Axial Systems Ltd, are pleased to announce a product that fulfils these requirements –
TREND from DeskTalk. This is a powerful enterprise network and systems
management tool for automated reporting and long term trend analysis.
Trend has the ability to collect network data from a variety of sources including
standard MIBs, proprietary MIBs and RMON agents. TREND stores this polled data
in a central database from which user-defined reports can be generated automatically
at regular intervals.

Scaleable from a single user environment up to enterprise wide management
structures, TREND has the flexibility to adapt and grow with a network to ensure that
all data on a network is harnessed into clear concise reports.
Because it supports standards, rather than just vendor specific products, TREND
provides a complete view of network performance enabling users to make calculated
decisions on how to improve processes.

Uniquely suited to both novices and experts, this package is extremely flexible.
With little prior training, users can obtain useful management reports, and once more
experienced, users are able to customise existing reports and create new ones.

By intelligently processing collected data such as response times, availability,
utilisation, inventory, resource usage, traffic counts and events, TREND can produce
more meaningful reports.

Axial Systems Ltd
+44 (0) 1628 418000

Reports can be created automatically or customised in a format to best suit the user.

Aggregating data and supplying statistical analysis provides an accurate baseline of typical network activity enabling users to see how current operations are performing, and forecast for the future.

The new TREND 3.5 automated System ReportPacks offer current and forthcoming support for:

- LAN
- Routers
- Servers
- WAN
- Cisco Routers
- NetScout
- Frame Relay
- RMON / RMON2

Features include:

- Polling policy based on pre-defined groups customised objects
- Pre-defined reports, allowing generation of reports without expertise
- True scaleability

- Point and click database administration

- Automated processing and managing of data
- Multiple, flexible report formats

- True client/server performance monitoring and reporting applications
- Grade of Service (GOS) report application

Axial Systems Ltd
+44 (0) 1628 418000

AXIAL

Find the story. How not to do it. A logo instead of a headline, a waffly first paragraph, the product announcement puffed unnecessarily in the second par. Too much unexplained jargon and poor layout, especially on the second page.

Marks out of ten: 3

Glossary of Press Terms

Art: US-originated term, now coming into UK vogue, meaning pictures, photos, diagrams and any other visual material for illustrating an article.

Back set: Subsequent section of a newspaper printed and folded separately. Like the Business and Review sections of the *Sunday Times* or *Observer*.

Banner: Usually means the name title at the top of the front page like *The Independent, Daily Mirror*, etc. Less often used as a term for a sensationally large headline.

Beat: A reporter's regular stamping ground — for example, the courts, Parliament, City, etc.

Bleed: Technique of making a picture run off the edge of the page.

Blow up: Technique of increasing (or decreasing) the size of a picture or other art (qv).

Body copy: Main text in a newspaper or magazine.

Broadsheet: Newspaper with large pages, such as *The Times* or *The Guardian*.

Byline: The author's name on an article.

Caption: Words that describe the contents of or accompany a picture. Usually set below or to the side of the picture.

Cast off: Technique of calculating the amount of space an article will take up.

Catchline: Key word at the top of each page of copy in article. Its purpose is to identify all the pages of the same article. Usually followed by the page number.

Centre spread: The centre pages of a newspaper or magazine.

Clipping: Article cut out of newspaper or magazine.

Column: Way in which a newspaper or magazine page is divided vertically.

Column measure: The width of the column, usually measured in ems (qv).

Columnist: Regular writer in newspaper or magazine normally promoted with a big byline (qv) and sometimes a picture.

Copy: General-purpose word for anything that has been written for a paper or magazine.

Copyright: The rights owned by the author of an article. Governed by complex UK and international legislation.

Copy taker: High-speed typist who takes down stories often dictated over the phone from reporters.

Copy taster: A sub-editor (qv) who reads all the copy and (most) press releases and reviews their news value.

Coverage: Term applied to the amount of space devoted by a publication to a particular topic.

Crop: Technique of editing a photograph or picture to exclude parts that are not to be published.

Cross-head: Small heading part of the way down a column.

Dateline: Rather hackneyed term which describes the place and date from which a story has come.

Deadline: Last time for copy to be delivered if it is to appear in the next issue or edition (qv) of a newspaper or magazine.

Defamation: Unfair and injurious comments or criticism of a person or organisation.

Diary: Literally a diary kept in the newsroom of most publications listing the events which have to be covered.

Dummy: Mock-up of a newspaper or magazine showing where the articles and advertisements are to be placed.

Edition: All the newspapers printed with the same contents. A daily or evening newspaper will have several editions, as stories are replaced and updated. A regional or local paper might have different geographical editions.

Editor: The boss of a newspaper or magazine. He sets the tone of the publication, hires the staff, decides what is published, and bears legal responsibility for everything published (including the advertisements).

Editorial: Article expressing the publication's opinion carried in most newspapers and magazines.

Em: The basic measurement of width in newspaper layouts. Normally one-sixth of an inch (known as the 12 point em).

En: Half an em.

Exclusive: An article which no other newspaper has got.

Feature: Article distinguished from a news report by exploring background or other issues. Can be of a light-hearted nature.

Filler: Short item used, normally, at the bottom of a column. Once beloved of the *Daily Telegraph*, still used in the *Reader's Digest*, but elsewhere falling out of fashion.

Flat plan: Diagram showing how the pages are arranged in a newspaper or magazine.

Fold: Half way down the page of, usually, a broadsheet paper where it is folded by the printing machinery. Editors try to ensure there is a telling headline 'above the fold'.

Folio: Term given to a page of copy.

Follow up: The next episode in a running story (qv).

Galley proof: Columns of text set in long columns for proof reading and layout.

Grid: Basic layout structure of a newspaper or magazine, defining the columns, spaces between columns, depth of columns, space at top and bottom of page and so on.

Hole: Space on a newspaper or magazine page which lacks copy or pictures and sometimes creates panic among sub-editors.

House style: Term given to the way different expressions will be printed in a publication in order to ensure consistency of spelling, punctuation, treatment of numbers, etc.

Intro: Word commonly used by journalists to denote the first two or three paragraphs of an article.

Kern: A printer's term for closing the space between letters in order to fit more into a line. Normally done with headlines which are just a little too long.

Layout: The way in which all the articles, pictures, etc are displayed on a page.

Leader: Another word given to an editorial (qv).

Literal: Simple error in text often caused by mistyping.

Make-up: The process of creating a layout (qv).

Masthead: Sometimes applied to the paper's name on the front page but also to the heading at the top of the leader (qv).

Morgue: Journalists' term for the library of press cuttings from which they research some stories.

News editor: The editorial executive who manages the team of front-line reporters and who, with the editor, determines news priorities for the newspaper or magazine.

Panel: Short article, often supplementing a longer piece, set in a panel on the page. See also *sidebar*.

Point: (1) The measure of height in typefaces. One point equals roughly $1/72$ of an inch. (2) Journalists' word for a full stop.

Press day: The day a publication's editorial and advertising content is sent to the printer. Not a good day to telephone journalists.

Press pack: Collection of press releases and other material such as photographs, brochures, etc.

Proof: Set text produced for checking.

Proof reader: Individual who checks proofs (qv).

Publisher: The executive on a newspaper or magazine responsible for the overall commercial success of the publication.

Pull-out: Section in a newspaper printed in such a way that it can be detached easily from the other pages.

Rewrite: A story rewritten, often by a sub-editor. Rewrites take place because the original is not up to standard and cannot be sub-edited into shape.

Running story: News item that develops from day to day — such as a murder hunt.

Scoop: Not seriously used these days by journalists who prefer the term 'exclusive' (Evelyn Waugh finished off 'scoop' in his book of the same name) but referring to an exclusive story.

Sidebar: A smaller story run alongside a larger piece, often based on an anecdote or example.

Spread: Two facing pages in a publication.

Standfirst: The words which describe or trail the contents of an article, sometimes called a blurb or lead-in.

Story: Commonly used term by journalists for a news article.

Strap: Small headline, often at the top of a page, describing the general contents of the page ie City, Sport, etc.

Stringer: Often freelance reporter covering a specific geographical area for national or regional newspapers.

Sub-editor: A journalist who edits copy and helps to fit it into the pages available, along with pictures, etc.

Tabloid: A newspaper with pages roughly half the size of a broadsheet (qv). Examples are *The Sun* and the *Daily Express*.

Further Reading

HELP WITH WRITING STYLE

Perfect Business Writing, Peter Bartram, Century Business (1993).
Mastering Business English, Michael Bennie, How To Books (3rd edition 1998).
Writing a Report, John Bowden, How To Books (4th edition 1998).
The Business Guide to Effective Writing, J. A. Fletcher and D. F. Gowing, Kogan Page (2nd edition 1987).
Business Writing Quick & Easy, Laura Brill, Mercury Books (2nd edition 1989).
Waterhouse on Newspaper Style, Keith Waterhouse, Viking (1989).

USEFUL REFERENCE

The Complete Spokesperson, a workbook for managers who meet the media, Peter Bartram and Colin Coulson-Thomas, Kogan Page (1991).
The Writer's Handbook, Macmillan, published annually.
Writer's and Artist's Yearbook, A & C Black, published annually.
Fowler's Modern English Usage, ed: Sir Ernest Gowers, Oxford (2nd edition 1965).
Roget's Thesaurus, Penguin Books (1998).
The Economist Pocket Style Book, Economist Publications (1986).

Useful Addresses

PRESS CUTTINGS EVALUATION SERVICE

Portfolio Metrica
  Russell Chambers
  The Piazza, Covent Garden
  London WC2E 8AP
  (0171) 240 6959 or 7447.

PRESS CUTTING AGENCIES

Durrant's Press Cuttings
  Discovery House,
  28-42 Banner Street
  London EC1Y 8QE
  (0171) 694 0200.

International Press Cutting Bureau
  224-236 Walworth Road
  London SE17 1JE
  (0171) 708 2113.

PIMS Press Cutting Service
  Pims House, Mildmay Avenue
  London N1 4RS
  (0171) 226 1000.

Romeike & Curtice Ltd
  Hale House
  Green Lanes
  London N13 5TQ
  (0181) 882 0155.

RADIO AND TV MONITORING AGENCIES

Broadcast Monitoring Company
89$^{1}/_{2}$ Worship Street
London EC2A 2BE
(0171) 247 1166.

PROFESSIONAL ASSOCIATIONS

Public Relations Consultants
Association
  Willow House
  Willow Place
  London SW1P 1JH
  (0171) 233 6026.

Institute of Public Relations
  The Old Trading House
  15 Northburgh Street
  London EC1V 0PR
  (0171) 253 5151.

Index